08/17

Please return this book on or before the date shown above. To renew go to www.essex.gov.uk/libraries, ring 0345 603 7628 or go to any Essex library.

Essex County Council

Oliver Warre

Essex County Council

3013021396135 1

Published in the United Kingdom by Eastdown Publishing, 2015

ISBN 978-0-9933122-0-5

Design and layout by Keith Rigley, Charlbury, Oxon
Set in Frutiger LT Std and Warnock Pro

Contents

Introduction

Hospitals are a constant presence in the lives of many people. The majority of us will start our lives in one, and almost all of us will be admitted to hospital at some point. Our children may be born there and many of us will die there. We are constantly bombarded with information, news and stories about hospitals. Some of our most popular films and television series are based in them.

Despite all this, when you arrive in hospital as a patient the environment is strange, people speak a language that you may not fully understand, and the daily routine is unfamiliar. You will have experiences unlike any you may have had before. There are unusual customs, traditions, hierarchies and dress codes. Going into hospital is in many ways like visiting a foreign land.

The hospital as a foreign land

We compare the hospital to a foreign land as a way of conveying the sense of bewilderment and confusion that many people feel when they go there. Patients in hospital often feel strangely vulnerable, and may temporarily lose much of their normal resourcefulness and assertiveness. This applies even to us as authors; we still feel nervous and vulnerable when we become patients ourselves.

The staff of the hospital will investigate your illness and, within the time they have available, explain the findings of your investigations, the choices you have, and the implications, risks and benefits of the treatments on offer. While they will be kind and try to explain everything, you may not always understand or remember who you spoke to, or exactly what they said. They will not generally have time to explain how the hospital system works or to provide the background information about health and healthcare that will help you make the best decisions for you and your family.

Why we decided to write this book

When visiting a foreign country we often buy a guide that explains its language, culture and customs, and that describes the places we may visit and the experiences we might have. The guide helps us take care of ourselves, gives advice on 'staying safe', and makes our experience more comprehensible. This book is your guide to the foreign land of the hospital. It provides clear, practical information about your journey and the investigations and treatments you may receive. At times, we use examples and stories from patients to describe how a particular aspect of healthcare feels and to give important tips on what helped them and their families.

We hope to help you work with the doctors, nurses and other clinicians as a true partner in your care. We hope to reassure you about the process of being in hospital while being clear about some of the risks. People who are better informed and who understand concepts such as choice, risk and benefit can work more effectively with their healthcare team to make the right decisions.

You may also sometimes need to understand the language of hospitals, which is full of strange terms, acronyms (like CPR, SHO and ITU) and historical words and phrases. It can sometimes feel as a patient – an 'outsider' – that these terms are there to make your visit as confusing as possible! We have purposely tried in this book to avoid as many as possible, but there are some which have necessarily crept in because you may hear them during your stay. We explain them as they occur in the book, but if doctors or other healthcare professionals use any words, phrases or acronyms that you do not understand while you are in hospital, do not hesitate to ask a member of staff what they mean.

People, patients, partners, families, friends and carers

We use a number of different terms when discussing people in hospital and those to whom they are close. We use the term 'patient' when we need to be absolutely clear who we are referring to, but otherwise try to use the terms 'person' or 'people' as much as we can. We have struggled to find the best way of talking about all the different people who might be close to a patient and involved in their care; these may include families of many different kinds, partners, carers, loved ones and friends. We realise that whatever words we use, we are always in danger of leaving someone out, as it is simply not possible to include every permutation of personal and social relationship. Most people have friends and family, but not all are able to rely on their support in times of illness or disability.

In some chapters, we describe scenarios in which the other people in our lives may be involved in key decisions, such as when decisions need to be made but the patients themselves are unconscious or too ill to participate. In all cases we have tried to keep references to 'family and friends' as generic as possible, and do not want to give the impression that we are making any assumptions about a typical family. In our many years of working in healthcare we have seen a vast range of 'family' lives, and would not presume that any one particular model would apply to any single reader. So whenever we mention family, friends, partners or carers, what we really mean is 'those to whom you are close and who you choose to involve in your care' – whoever they may be.

The scope of the book

This book is mainly aimed at adult patients and their families, friends and carers. We have included a chapter on children in hospital, but we recognise that a separate guide for children is probably needed. We have not covered maternity services (although much of the information is relevant to any woman who requires medical or surgical help during her pregnancy or labour), nor have we covered hospital care for mental illness, which we believe also requires a separate guide. Hospitals and other organisations provide leaflets and websites devoted to specific conditions and investigations. These can be extremely useful and we recommend that you look at these. However, this book has a rather different purpose, which is to explain how hospitals work in general, no matter what your particular disease, and how to cope with this unfamiliar environment. We cannot be entirely comprehensive, in much the same way that no travel guide can include every restaurant, hotel and attraction.

The guide is most relevant to hospitals in the United Kingdom National Health Service (NHS), which covers England, Wales, Scotland and Northern Ireland (although the systems in each are slightly different). However, a lot of the clinical information is quite generic and should be equally relevant to people in private hospitals or being treated in other countries.

How to use this book

You may be reading this book as someone who is about to go into hospital to have a planned investigation or treatment. You may have a longstanding illness that occasionally requires hospital treatment. You may have a relative or friend who has recently been admitted to hospital. In every case you can approach the book in the same way, which is to read the sections that are most relevant to you. We have structured it so that, just like a travel guide, you can read some general background information and then move to the sections that are of particular interest and relevance to you. We suggest that most of Chapters 1–6 are relevant to everyone, in that they explain some important background about the experience of being a patient and the way hospitals work. Chapters 7–9 help you understand who the staff are and what they do, and also introduce you to the main areas of the hospital. You should then select those of Chapters 10–17 that are relevant to you. It is, for instance, only worth reading about endoscopy if you are actually going to have one! We suggest that everyone should read Chapters 18–22, as it is important for you to do what you can do to help keep yourself safe and well in hospital. You will recover more quickly if you keep yourself as active as possible, keep in touch with family and friends, and generally try to continue with as much of your ordinary life as possible. Chapters 23–25 cover some specific topics that are only relevant to certain groups of people, and finally Chapter 26 discusses leaving hospital after an inpatient stay.

We hope you find the guide useful and that it makes your journey through the hospital easier.

Acknowledgements

Many people have helped in the writing of this book. Some have provided specialist material for chapters, some have contributed personal stories, and some have been kind enough to read and comment on sections of the book. We would particularly like to thank: Frances Akor, Kerem Atalar, Elizabeth Banham, Ben Byrne, Lucy Cook, Mark Gilchrist, Nicola Gray, Jean Harris, Fran Husson, Seetal Jheeta, Bob Klaber, Susy Long, Anna Martin, Luke Moore, Kathy Nairne, Jude Partridge, Lucy Pickard, Joc Potter, Lizzie Provis, Fiona Reed, Anne Richardson, Emily Thompson, Helen Thurley, Jim Vincent and Linda Warren.

We would also like to thank Keith Rigley for designing and setting the book so elegantly, Andy Hopkins for design management, and Joc Potter for assiduous and thoughtful editing and for being our guide in the foreign land of publishing.

About the authors

Oliver Warren

I am a consultant in general and colorectal surgery at Chelsea and Westminster Hospital in London and an honorary lecturer in the Centre for Patient Safety and Service Quality at Imperial College London. Since graduating in 2001, I have worked in a variety of hospitals, ranging from big central London teaching hospitals to smaller local hospitals, and in many different specialties, including emergency medicine, trauma and orthopaedics, cardiothoracic surgery and general surgery. I have worked outside the NHS, in a large hospital in Sydney, where I spent a year as a senior trainee, and in a non-clinical role in the UK government. Despite being relatively fit and well, I have had seven operations, all requiring admission to hospital, and many more visits after sports injuries, so I have a good idea of what it feels like to be a patient. I am struck by the huge variations in the experience of patients, even within the same department or hospital, and how much these experiences are shaped by the behaviours of those professionals with whom they come into contact. Rarely a week goes by when I don't help a friend, colleague or family member navigate an increasingly complex healthcare system in the hope of improving their quality of care; this book is an attempt to do this for more patients than I can by myself.

Bryony Dean Franklin

I am a pharmacist by background, and although I have worked in community pharmacy and the pharmaceutical industry for short periods I have been based in hospitals for most of my working life. I am currently Professor of Medication Safety at University College London School of Pharmacy, Visiting Professor at Imperial College, and a hospital pharmacist at Imperial College Healthcare NHS Trust in west London, where I am also Chair of the Centre for Patient Safety and Service Quality. I am interested in developing and testing ways of making healthcare safer, particularly in relation to medicines, and in how we can better involve patients and their families in their own healthcare. I am lucky to be fairly healthy, but I have had a few hospital admissions and know a little about what it feels like to be at the other end of the hospital bed. I have also helped 'translate' hospital terminology, customs and practices for many of my friends, family and acquaintances, and am often struck by how the hospital experience can be much more positive when you understand a little more about what is going on, what to expect, and what you and your family and friends can do to help.

Charles Vincent

I trained as a clinical psychologist and worked in the NHS for several years before becoming a researcher. Since 1985, I have carried out research on medical error and risks to patients, and studied how to improve the safety and quality of healthcare. I have always been particularly concerned with how patients can be supported during stressful experiences in healthcare. I became a Professor of Psychology at University College London before moving to Imperial College London in 2002. I have written many scientific papers on risk and safety in healthcare and a book on Patient Safety (2nd edition 2010). For ten years I worked in the Department of Surgery and Cancer at Imperial College London and was Director of the Imperial Centre for Patient Safety & Service Quality. My office was in a hospital, so I was very close to all the daily activities and still have many clinical friends and colleagues. I am now Professor of Psychology at the University of

Oxford. I see hospitals partly as a researcher who is very familiar with the environment, but also as a lay person who is not part of the clinical world. At the time of writing I am fortunate not to have been admitted to hospital for decades. In recent years, however, I spent many hours in hospitals with each of my parents before they died, while we attempted to navigate the healthcare system together.

Being a patient

CHAPTER ONE

The wonders and challenges of modern healthcare

In 1948, when the National Health Service (NHS) came into being, medical practice was very different from the service we have today. Being a doctor or nurse in the 1940s was demanding and challenging, but it was also much simpler. There was less to know, the pace of investigation and treatment was slower, there were fewer specialists to deal with and far fewer decisions to make. Antibiotics, insulin and other drugs were available, but the total number of medicines in use was very small. Surgeons could deal with simple injuries, but serious trauma was usually fatal. Patients 50 years ago had lower expectations, fewer options, fewer decisions to make and much less access to information about their illness. They were also less likely to question decisions made by their doctors and less likely to be actively involved in their own care.

In the early days of the NHS patients were admitted to hospital for considerably longer periods of time, and were looked after by small teams of doctors and nurses. Most hospitals provided a similar range of treatments, so the need to travel further afield to get highly specialised treatments rarely arose. When Anthony Vincent (Charles's father) had an operation to remove the cartilage from his knee in the 1960s, he was in hospital for a week. He saw the same doctor and nurses every day, had a long operation and a large scar on his leg, and recovered slowly from his hospital bed. Today the procedure takes around an hour and requires a few tiny incisions about a centimetre long, and he would hopefully go home the same day.

The wonders of medicine in the 21st century

Healthcare is evolving at an astonishing rate. Many childhood and infectious diseases can now be prevented and many previously fatal diseases, such as breast cancer, can be treated effectively and often completely cured. A child born in 2015 can expect to live ten years longer than someone who was born in 1965, and one third of children born in 2015 will probably see their 100th birthday.

If you suffered a heart attack in the 1950s and survived long enough to get to hospital, you were treated with bed rest and medication that we now know to be relatively ineffective. There was no echocardiogram ('echo') to see if the heart muscle was damaged and there was no angiography (a technique that provides real-time pictures of the arteries of the heart while the heart beats). If you have a heart attack today, a battery of highly sensitive tests is available to diagnose the problem precisely. Treatment can be given through a small incision in the groin, from which a wire is passed to the heart. A small balloon is opened inside the damaged arteries to clear any blockage. You can arrive at a hospital at death's door and be home two days later feeling shaken but essentially fit and healthy. For those affected, and their families, such treatment is little short of miraculous.

New technologies are continually pushing the boundaries of what can be achieved in investigations and treatment. New ways of viewing the internal organs of the body (such as PET, CT and MRI scanners, explained in Chapter 13) allow rapid diagnosis of disease in ways that were unthinkable 20 years ago. Advances in surgical technologies have transformed many operations. In

1980 removal of the gallbladder to take out gallstones and prevent their recurrence required a large cut on the right side of the abdomen and a week in hospital to recover. Now around 95% of these operations are done with keyhole surgery (see Chapter 15) and about one third of patients go home on the same day. An aortic aneurysm (an abnormal swelling of the biggest blood vessel in the body) could previously only be repaired with a major abdominal operation, from which it would take weeks to recover. Now many patients undergo a procedure called an endovascular repair, which uses only a small incision in the groin to access the body. No major surgery is required, there is very little scarring, and the patient can usually go home the next day.

Challenges and changes to healthcare

While this progress has been remarkable, the achievements of modern medicine have brought a number of challenges in their wake and have changed the way healthcare needs to be delivered. These are some of the changes that have the most important implications for patients:

Each individual hospital doctor knows more and more about less and less. Medical knowledge is so vast, and is changing so quickly, that no one can fully understand even a small proportion of it. This means that hospital doctors and other professionals have to specialise and concentrate on particular diseases and treatments.

Teams of people, not individuals, deliver healthcare. The days of the single all-knowing consultant standing at the end of the bed are over. Teams are now essential and almost certainly offer higher standards of care. However, information has to be passed between all these people to ensure that everyone remains informed. Patients have to see many different healthcare professionals and discuss their care with more people than in the past.

Decisions about your care are also made by teams of people.
These teams are made up of members of different professions
and specialties to make sure that all viewpoints and perspectives
are considered. This is valuable, but it sometimes means that final
decisions on your treatment options will have to wait until the
team can all come together and discuss your case.

Clinicians now specialise in the procedures they undertake.
Surgeons used to carry out a wide range of operations on all
parts of the body. In one day the same surgeon would have
performed operations on the bladder, breast, thyroid and aorta.
Today this would involve four different surgeons in four different
operating theatres. Some doctors may specialise in just one or
two very specific diseases or operations.

*Specialist treatment is often provided in a small number of
hospitals.* For instance, a very small number of young children
require specialist heart surgery. The best units tend to be those
that do the highest number of operations, and are situated in
hospitals which have other specialist services for children. Experts
in this area have therefore recommended fewer centres, but bigger, better equipped and better staffed ones. This means that
some children may need to be transferred between hospitals and
treated further from their home. If you or your loved one needs
very specialist treatment, it is generally worth travelling, even
long distances, to receive the very best care.

*New treatments are developed all the time but may not
yet have enough evidence to support their routine use.* The
media often report on 'wonder-drugs' or 'miracle treatments',
but this is rarely the reality. People may read about exciting new
treatments but then find that they are not routinely available and
very possibly that the benefits have been exaggerated. Most new
treatments are reviewed by expert bodies such as the National
Institute for Clinical and Healthcare Excellence (NICE) in England,

which decide if there is sufficient evidence of both effectiveness and cost benefits to society to recommend them.

Expectations have risen. The last 50 years have brought major technological changes, but also major social changes that have transformed our attitudes to healthcare. Patients, rightly, expect more from healthcare and more from the people who provide it. Sometimes, however, these expectations may become too high. Clinicians frequently have to explain that the investigation or treatment that the patient wants might not benefit them, or that the risks involved may outweigh any potential benefit. Some people now find it hard to accept illness, disability and death as ordinary facts of life.

Implications for patients

When the NHS started in 1948, there were relatively few effective treatments and healthcare was comparatively simple. Doctors knew most of what there was to know, and advised patients what they should do. People moved home far less often, and generally lived in smaller communities. As a result, their family doctor knew them well, and was a key figure in the community.

Healthcare is now highly effective, but it is also complex and carries significant risks. Doctors and others can only be expert in tiny areas of medicine. Hospital stays are much shorter and more care is delivered in the home. What are the implications of these changes for patients?

Patients now have more responsibility for their care. This is good in the sense that you have more say in your care, but also harder because you may have more decisions to make.

Patients need to participate in their care and work with the doctors, nurses and others as partners. You need to understand your care as much as possible because you may be asked to make decisions that previously would have been made for you.

Patients should keep their own records. You will help yourself and the healthcare professionals looking after you if you keep records of the medicines you take and of the investigations and treatments you have undergone.

Patients' values and preferences are important and need to be explained to the doctor. Only you can know what is most important to you and sometimes personal preference is the deciding factor between two treatment options.

There is a wealth of information available on the internet. Reading about your disease and its treatment can be very helpful, and allows you to understand the options available. However, you should also bear in mind that information on the internet is of variable quality, and the best decision is likely to emerge from discussing these options with your doctor and working out what is right for you. We provide a list of useful and reliable websites in the Appendix at the end of this book.

Patients, families and carers should be aware that doctors, nurses, pharmacists and other healthcare staff are human beings who can and do sometimes make mistakes. Patient safety is a priority and a core responsibility for all hospitals and all healthcare professionals. However, patients and their families can also play a part. Throughout this book we will suggest what you can do to keep yourself and your family safe in hospital.

CHAPTER TWO

Becoming a patient

Almost all of us will be admitted to hospital at some time in our lives, some of us many times. Being in hospital is inevitably a difficult experience – because we are ill and because the hospital itself is potentially an unfamiliar and disturbing environment. Some of the most significant experiences of our lives, both positive and negative, will occur in hospital. There may be sadness as parents or close friends die, or traumatic experiences of injury, but we may also experience extraordinary release and liberation from disease. Broken limbs, which would have crippled us in earlier centuries, are mended, allowing us to return to our normal functions within a few months. After years of dialysis, we may receive a new kidney and, in effect, a new life. We have a heart attack and are minutes from death, but can be treated and back home in a few days. Being a patient can be both difficult and wonderful.

The challenge of being a patient

Hospitals are familiar to us from television dramas, movies and documentaries, which provide astonishingly detailed descriptions of even major surgery, and comprehensive accounts of the experience of illness. Unlimited information, of exceedingly variable quality, can also be found on the internet. However, very little of this information tells you how the hospital actually works, what it will be like when you get there, or how you are likely to feel while you are there. Being in hospital can be a particularly difficult experience even for people who are generally very strong and confident. These are some of the main reasons:

You are ill. Even when you have an ordinary cold, you do not concentrate so well. You forget things, and quite ordinary tasks and responsibilities become worrying and burdensome. All this is magnified hugely if you are more seriously ill.

Healthcare can be very confusing, even to people who work in the system. Twenty years ago you would have been looked after by one or two doctors and a small team of nurses. Nowadays numerous people, from a wide range of professions, may come to see you. It is very difficult to keep track of who they are and what they do.

Many of the experiences can feel embarrassing. People you only met ten minutes ago are touching you and examining you with an intimacy that in any other setting would be unthinkable. As a patient you have to put aside, temporarily, your usual requirements for privacy. Clinicians try to preserve your dignity as much as they can, but this is not always possible; the loss of your personal boundaries can be unsettling.

Some diseases and some treatments change the way you look, sometimes permanently. Scars, swellings, hair loss, weight gain or weight loss and other changes to your body can change the way you feel about yourself as a person and your relationships with others. Your self-esteem may be affected.

You may be worried not only by your own illness but by its impact on your family, friends and work life. Who will look after your children? What will happen to that job interview you have to attend, the project you promised to deliver? Who will look after your pets?

You may also, in a way that is hard to describe, feel less significant than usual or less capable of acting for yourself. Somehow much of your experience, your resourcefulness and your sense of yourself as a person has been left outside the hospital door. You may not quite recognise this person that you have temporarily become. Here, a patient describes her experience.

....

▲▲ *The first time I went into hospital, from the moment I arrived on the ward, I had the strange experience of seeming to lose my normal adult identity.*

First of all a wristband is put on you with your name on, and then you're asked to undress and get into your night clothes to get into bed. After this, various other procedures, such as taking your temperature, are likely to follow. All of this is well intentioned, but it made me feel like a child. I had to surrender control over my life on a temporary basis and become 'a patient'. If you're very seriously ill this is not so likely to be a problem but if, like me, you come into hospital for an operation feeling relatively well beforehand, you may find this disturbing.

At the same time the nurses and doctors and other staff become powerful people like parents. Since you're now dependent on how they behave towards you, you can feel very sensitive to their tone or manner. I certainly found myself becoming more emotionally volatile – more easily becoming tearful or angry. This surprised me. **▼▼**

....

Your rights and responsibilities

When we go shopping, stay in a hotel or travel we have certain rights as a citizen and a consumer. All NHS patients are covered by the NHS Constitution, which gives a very clear explanation of your rights as a patient. Other healthcare systems have similar statements, although not always as comprehensive. Knowing your rights should empower you and tell you what you can expect from your care. For instance, you have a right to be treated with respect. You should not have to put up with someone being rude

> **Box 1** *Your rights as a hospital patient: some examples from the NHS Constitution*
>
> - You have the right to be treated with dignity and respect, in accordance with your human rights.
> - You have the right not to be unlawfully discriminated against in the provision of NHS services, including on grounds of gender, race, religion or belief, sexual orientation, disability or age.
> - You have the right to access services within maximum waiting times, or for the NHS to take all reasonable steps to offer you a range of alternative providers if this is not possible.
> - The NHS commits to make the transition as smooth as possible when you are referred between services, and to include you in relevant discussions.
> - You have the right to expect NHS organisations to monitor, and make efforts to improve, the quality of healthcare they commission or provide.
> - The NHS also commits to ensure that services are provided in a clean and safe environment that is fit for purpose, based on national best practice.
> - The NHS commits to continuous improvement in the quality of services you receive, identifying and sharing best practice in quality of care and treatments.
> - You have the right to drugs and treatments that have been recommended for use in the NHS, if your doctor says they are clinically appropriate for you.

to you, no matter how senior or experienced they may be. We have summarised some of the main rights set out in the NHS Constitution in Box 1. You can find a copy of the full document on the internet, or ask for it at the hospital or a local library.

Please do read these rights, or at least our summary of them, and refer to them when you need to. These are expectations that you should have of your hospital and those looking after you, and expectations that we as a society have of each other when using health services.

Box 2 *Your responsibilities as a patient: some examples from the NHS Constitution*

- The NHS belongs to all of us. There are things that we can all do for ourselves and for one another to help it work effectively, and to ensure that NHS resources are used responsibly.
- You should recognise that you can make a significant contribution to your own and your family's good health and well-being, and take some personal responsibility for this.
- You should register with a GP practice – the main point of access to NHS care.
- You should treat NHS staff and other patients with respect.
- You should provide accurate information about your health, condition and status.
- You should keep appointments or cancel within a reasonable time. Receiving treatment within the maximum waiting times may be compromised unless you do.
- You should follow the course of treatment which you have agreed, and talk to your clinician if you find this difficult.
- You should participate in all important public health programmes, such as vaccination.
- You should ensure that those closest to you are aware of your wishes about organ donation.
- You should give feedback – both positive and negative – about the treatment and care you have received, including any adverse reactions you may have had.

The NHS Constitution states that the NHS belongs to all of us and that we have a right to a good standard of care. However, we also have responsibilities as patients. For instance, we should treat NHS staff with respect. We should not waste or disrupt the care provided, because we are then taking resources away from someone else who needs help. Our responsibilities as patients are summarised in Box 2 (see above).

Sources of support

Being a patient is often tough, but this is only one side of the picture. We are all likely to be anxious about going into hospital and the authors of this book are no exceptions. However, we also know that people cope with very serious illnesses and emerge with their lives intact and even with their happiness and faith in others enhanced. People are remarkably resilient and resourceful. Human beings constantly astonish themselves and others with their ability to adapt, to fight and to endure in order to ensure that they come out of the other side of their illness. As a patient you have some very important sources of help and guidance available to you:

Staff will provide support. The staff are there to investigate your illness and to treat you. However, that is too narrow a way of describing their work and responsibilities. Their job is also to help you as a person by supporting, caring, cajoling and nursing you back to health.

Your family, friends or carers can provide a great deal of emotional and practical support. Let them help you and take over your responsibilities for a while.

Other patients, in the hospital and elsewhere, can be an enormous source of advice, encouragement and hope. Patient groups, set up by those who have suffered from the same condition or undergone the same treatment, can be invaluable.

Often it feels as though no one else can possibly understand how you may feel, unless they have gone through that experience themselves.

Some practical ways to support yourself

Throughout this book we will be suggesting questions to ask, ways of supporting and providing comfort to yourself and others, and practical things to do in particular situations. However, it is worth starting now with some straightforward principles and suggestions:

Ask questions if you want to. If you do not understand something that is important to you, ask a member of staff to explain.

Ask a friend or family member to speak for you. If you need to ask questions but do not feel strong enough or well enough yourself, then ask someone to be with you and to speak on your behalf.

Do not be shy or concerned about bothering staff. If you feel something is wrong, if you have been misunderstood, or if you feel you are not receiving the care that you should, speak to a member of staff about it. Staff rely on you to communicate concerns to them, as it helps them monitor your condition.

Write things down or ask a friend to write things down for you. If you will be in hospital for a few days, it may be useful to keep a diary of what has happened, who you saw, what medicines you were given and other information.

Look after yourself. Bring into hospital your favourite photographs, magazines, books, music or anything else that you enjoy and that reminds you of your life at home.

Understanding what is happening and why it is happening will make the experience of hospital easier to bear and easier to manage. Using this book and other resources to prepare yourself will make the hospital a much less confusing place. 'Knowledge conquers fear' is a motto used in one of our local emergency departments and we believe this book fits in with that ethos.

Going to
hospital

CHAPTER THREE

Reasons to go to hospital

Why might you be admitted to hospital? This may initially seem obvious – because you are ill. But people are admitted to hospital for a whole host of different reasons. Some people are immediately and obviously ill. For instance, a person with serious pneumonia or who has just been hit by a car needs urgent admission and medical care. But people who are generally healthy may also be admitted for investigations or some form of treatment. A lot of pregnant women attend hospital and give birth there, and fortunately only a very small number are ill – the rest are thriving! There is another reason why the simple label of being 'ill' or 'unwell' is not always helpful – it can make you consider yourself incapable or disempowered even if this is not actually the case. People also respond very differently to their illnesses, some regarding a mild viral infection as a reason to stop all their normal activities while others carry on through serious pain and disability.

To understand why people are admitted to hospital and by what route, we need to consider some different categories of illness.

Acute and chronic conditions

We first distinguish between 'acute' and 'chronic' conditions. Acute conditions are those which develop relatively quickly. Injuries resulting from a fall, a heart attack or a stroke (increasingly referred to as a 'brain attack') are regarded as acute conditions. In contrast, chronic conditions are longstanding illnesses. People sometimes use the word 'chronic' incorrectly, thinking it means serious or severe. However, this is not the case: chronic means persistent or long term, and chronic conditions may be relatively minor or more serious.

Acute conditions

Acute conditions are newly arising conditions which were not there before and can happen at any time. Some acute conditions, such as a heart attack or stroke, are obviously severe and require urgent hospital treatment. Other acute conditions do not generally require a visit to hospital. A general practitioner (GP) for instance, may diagnose and treat a nasty ear infection, tonsillitis or cellulitis on the leg (a kind of skin infection). Sometimes the GP will send people with acute illnesses to hospital for more investigations or treatment, and if the problem is really urgent, may send them direct to the emergency department (ED). Common acute problems for which people visit the ED are listed in Box 3.

> **Box 3** *Examples of acute conditions requiring attendance at the emergency department*
>
> - Myocardial infarction (heart attack)
> - Pneumonia (a serious infection of the lungs)
> - Trauma and injuries
> - Bowel obstruction
> - Severe bleeding
> - Anaphylaxis (a severe form of sudden allergic reaction)
> - Stroke
> - Appendicitis

A significant proportion of patients attending the emergency department have injuries or 'trauma'. Trauma can range from injury to a single limb, for example a broken hip caused by a fall, to major 'multi-system' trauma, which might occur when someone is hit by a car or badly beaten.

Once treated, acute conditions generally resolve completely, often without any form of long-lasting damage or complications. A classic example is a case of appendicitis that suddenly develops in a young person. They will have an operation, probably going home sometime in the following one or two days, and the problem should be completely resolved. They will continue to live the same healthy, normal life that they led previously. In other cases, people may be left with a residual problem or disability. For instance, someone may suffer an acute head injury and find that their memory and ability to concentrate never quite return to previous levels.

Chronic conditions

About 15 million people in England have a chronic condition. Chronic conditions are those for which there may well be treatments, but there is currently no cure. Examples include diabetes, chronic obstructive pulmonary disease, HIV, arthritis and hypertension. The life of a person with a chronic condition is forever altered – there is no 'return to normal'. However, the majority of people with chronic conditions continue to live happy and fulfilling lives.

Chronic conditions are on the increase, which may sound alarming but is due in part to the ability of modern medicine to treat people successfully. This means that some conditions that were once fatal have become chronic conditions that people can live with for a long time. Unfortunately, the other reason that some chronic conditions are on the increase is because of our lifestyles. For instance, type 2 diabetes is associated with a diet high in refined sugar, obesity and a sedentary lifestyle; lung cancer and chronic lung diseases are often caused by smoking. We as a society need to do more to prevent these conditions, or the costs of healthcare will become too high for us to afford in the future.

The vast majority of chronic conditions are managed in the community by GPs. However, a GP may decide that a patient requires specialist assessment or treatment. For instance, someone with diabetes may not be able to control their blood sugar level despite the best efforts of the GP and the patient, or a person with migraine may find that the attacks are becoming more severe or more frequent despite the use of medication. On those occasions, the GP may refer the patient to hospital for further investigation or specialist advice. Chronic conditions may also worsen to the extent that the patient requires admission to hospital because they are too ill to remain at home. A patient with cancer, for instance, may need to be admitted to manage their pain or other symptoms.

'Acute on chronic' conditions

Chronic conditions are, by definition, long-standing illnesses. However, many of them can 'flare up' or be complicated by another condition, including a condition which might not be as serious or as problematic in other people. This is another potential reason for someone with a chronic condition to be admitted to hospital. An example of this would be a person with chronic obstructive pulmonary disease (COPD, a disease of the lungs) who generally lives in their own home, managing their illness with a range of medication and occasional home oxygen. People with this illness are particularly prone to chest infections, and if they get an infection, their already damaged lungs will be more seriously affected. They then often require an admission to hospital for high doses of antibiotics, possibly supplemented with other treatments. When their condition has improved, they can return home and their GP can continue to help monitor, support and treat their condition.

Why are people admitted to hospital?

People may therefore be admitted due to acute, chronic or acute on chronic conditions. We have mainly described emergency admissions above, but sometimes people have a planned admission to hospital. These are often referred to as 'elective' admissions. Patients 'elect' to go into hospital and are given an admission appointment for investigations or treatment. Examples are most varicose vein operations, knee replacements or regular blood transfusions for people with anaemias. Elective admissions are discussed in more detail in Chapter 5. In contrast, emergency admissions occur when a person suddenly becomes unwell and requires unplanned hospital care; these are discussed in Chapter 6.

Whatever the nature of the condition, and whether admission is elective or an emergency, there are a number of reasons for being admitted to hospital:

You are too unwell to stay safely at home. Some illnesses are so serious that they require frequent or even continuous medical and nursing support. For instance, you might need treatment in the intensive care unit to supplement your breathing and support the functioning of your kidneys and circulation. You clearly need to be in hospital. Alternatively, you may be recovering from an operation or intervention. If you have had a three-hour anaesthetic to perform major abdominal surgery, your body will take time to recover. You will initially be too weak to look after yourself, so you need to stay in hospital until you have recovered.

You feel ill, but your doctor does not know why. Even if your doctor is not seriously worried by your condition, they may nevertheless wish to make an accurate assessment of what is wrong with you. For instance, many people with chest pain are admitted for short periods to have specific tests that allow the

doctors to be absolutely sure that the cause is not a heart attack
or a blood clot in the lung. Once these have been ruled out, the
patient can leave.

You require urgent investigations. You may require investigations and treatment that could potentially be given as an outpatient. However, even if you are not very ill your doctors may
decide to admit you to hospital to have the investigations. There
are various reasons for this:

- *Speed.* Tests can be conducted much more quickly if you are
  staying in hospital and can move from one investigation to
  another. If the medical team feel that there is a possibility of
  something serious, they will want to get the answer as quickly
  as possible
- *Patient mobility or frailty.* A fit person may be happy to come
  to hospital several times to have a series of tests. However, a
  frail older person who lives alone simply could not manage
  this. It is wiser for them to be admitted to hospital until all the
  tests are done.
- *The nature of the test.* Some investigations require blood tests
  or urine tests every few hours over a day or two, or require
  you to take special medicines. It may be more practical to be in
  hospital for the duration of such tests.

*You require specialist nursing care, physiotherapy, occu-
pational therapy and/or rehabilitation.* Sometimes, doctors are the last people you need! If you have had a stroke and
are now recovering, the most important people to bring you
back to health are the speech and language therapists and the
physiotherapists. You will have intensive sessions with these
professionals at least once a day. People do better if this is provided in a special intensive environment, so you may stay on the
stroke unit until your rehabilitation is complete or can continue
at home.

You require specialist medication or blood products that require constant monitoring or nursing input. Some medication, such as blood products or chemotherapy, needs to be given slowly over 24 hours or requires monitoring while it is being given. You may therefore have a planned admission for a couple of days to receive treatment, and then go home.

Social reasons and safety. There are times when whatever brought the patient into hospital leaves them with a permanent problem. This is particularly true for frail older people. You may have been coping perfectly well at home, perhaps with care and support provided, but then suffer an injury which leaves you less fit and less mobile. Perhaps you are not able to wash or dress yourself, and need a level of care for which there is no provision in your own home. The treatment may be straightforward and not last very long. However, you need to remain in hospital until an appropriate place can be found for you, such as a residential or nursing home. (Some of these issues are discussed further in Chapter 26.)

We believe, as do most clinicians, that patients should only be in hospital if they really need to be. It is therefore helpful to understand why you might be in hospital, and why you have been admitted. It is equally important to be able to take an active role in deciding when you can go home. Unless there are good reasons to stay in hospital, you are much better off at home. At home you are in your own environment, can eat and drink exactly when you wish, can sleep in your own bed, and have the support of your friends and family. These make you feel better and ensure your independence. So if you think that you, or the loved one you are visiting, do not need to stay in hospital, we urge you to ask the doctors looking after you why you are still there. Could you go home and come back another time for more tests or treatments? Can the care you are receiving be delivered in the community or in your own home? People should, as far as possible, always live in their own homes and be treated in their own environment.

CHAPTER FOUR

An outpatient appointment

Many people will attend hospital for an outpatient appointment at some point in their lives. These appointments can be for a wide range of health-related issues, but have one thing in common, which is that the patient is accessing more specialised care than they would receive from their general practitioner (GP). Examples might include someone with a skin condition being referred to a dermatology clinic because they have not responded to treatment given by their GP, or a GP seeking an opinion from a surgeon on whether or not a knee replacement would benefit a patient with bad arthritis.

This chapter is designed to help prepare you for any outpatient appointment by providing some advice on why you might need one, what to expect, what to do beforehand, and what to do when you are there. It offers help on how to make the most of your time with the doctor, nurse or other healthcare professional who you see during your visit.

Why do I need a hospital appointment?

If you are advised to attend a hospital outpatient appointment, you might be wondering why you need to see another doctor when you have your own GP. While your GP is very knowledgeable in most fields of medicine, they cannot be an expert in every field. GPs have a breadth of knowledge, rather than being specialists in one specific area. For example, if you are diagnosed with diabetes, in most cases your GP will be able to help you manage this. However, in some cases they might also want you to see a doctor called an endocrinologist, who specialises in the treatment of diabetes and similar conditions. Getting additional management from hospital specialists helps you and your GP to ensure that you are receiving the best treatment.

How will I get an appointment?

There are two main types of hospital appointment.

'New' appointments

If this is the first time that you are being seen in a particular clinic, your GP has probably decided that you may benefit from seeing a hospital specialist. However, there are other routes to an outpatient appointment. You may have been referred after a visit to a hospital emergency department by one of the doctors there, or occasionally a specialist in another area may ask for you to be seen by a colleague. These referrals between hospital colleagues used to be far more common, but recent health policy changes have added an extra step to the process. Previously if a surgeon wished you to see a heart specialist before a big operation, to ensure your heart was functioning well, they simply wrote to the specialist asking for them to see you in their outpatient clinic. The surgeon now frequently has to write to your GP, asking them to write to the heart specialist. This change is designed to place more power with the GPs, giving them more control of healthcare resources. However, it can potentially inconvenience patients and it adds extra steps to an already complex process.

If your GP has decided to refer you to a hospital, in England you can usually choose the hospital that is most convenient for you via the NHS Choose and Book system. This also allows you to book the specific date and time. You may be able to do this in the GP surgery, or from home by telephone or online. In other cases, you will receive a letter with an appointment which you will be able to rearrange if it is not convenient. At the time of writing the longest you should wait after being referred by your GP until you start hospital treatment is 18 weeks in England; this number is 26 weeks in Wales and 12 in Scotland. However, wherever possible the waiting time will be much less than this. If you feel that you have been waiting too long for an appointment, or are concerned that your referral has been somehow lost or delayed, you should contact your GP surgery.

Follow-up appointments

If you have already seen a specialist, they may wish to see you again to ensure that you are progressing well and that any intervention they have made in your care has been effective. This may be after an initial outpatient appointment, as described above, or following a hospital admission. For instance, you may have had an outpatient appointment with a respiratory physician who started you on a new inhaler to control your asthma; the physician will want to see you again four weeks later to check how effective it has been. Alternatively, you may have had a significant operation and have now been discharged home. The team who operated on you will want to review your progress a few weeks after the operation to see how you are getting on. Both of these are 'follow-up' appointments and will be made by the specialist hospital team looking after you, not by your GP.

Preparing for your appointment

If you have not been to the hospital before, it is definitely worth planning ahead (see Box 4). Hospital parking is often limited and costly, so public transport may be a better option, particularly in large cities. If you need assistance with getting to the hospital, discuss this with your GP or the hospital and they may be able to arrange transport for you. However, not all patients qualify for free patient transport, so you may need to ask a friend or relative to take you. Hospitals can be very large, with several buildings, so make sure you know in advance where you need to go and how to get there. Most hospitals have maps and transport advice on their websites.

There are additional reasons for taking a friend or relative with you. It can be very difficult to remember all the information that a doctor or other specialist tells you. A companion can help to remember things, and can write down key information during and after your appointment. It can also be comforting having someone with you if you have to wait for your appointment or for further investigations. Sadly, there are occasions when the news you receive may not be good and having a friend by your side can be very helpful. At the very least, they can go to the coffee shop to get you a drink; otherwise you might not be there when they call you in for your appointment!

Box 4 *Suggestions to help a trip to outpatients go smoothly*

- Plan your hospital visit a little ahead of time.
- Take public transport if possible, removing the stress of parking.
- Remember to take your admission letter with you.
- Be prepared for delays – take something to read.
- Jot down your past medical history and any medication you take beforehand.
- Write down any questions you wish to ask beforehand.
- Take a friend or relative if possible.
- Ask where you can get more information or help.

We encourage you, ahead of your appointment, to think about what questions you may want to ask, and to write them down to help guide the conversation during the appointment.

It is easy to forget otherwise, especially if you are feeling a bit stressed or rushed.

Where do I go when I get to the hospital?

Remember to take your admission letter with you, because this will state clearly which clinic you need to go to. Show it to the main reception desk and they will direct you. It is easy to get lost walking around a hospital and the staff are well accustomed to being stopped and asked for directions, so do not hesitate to ask anyone wearing a name badge for help. If you need a wheelchair or other assistance, just ask at the main reception.

What happens when I get to the clinic?

The first thing to do when you arrive at the outpatient clinic is to tell the receptionist that you have arrived. Before seeing the doctor or nurse you may be weighed or asked to provide a urine sample. This might seem unnecessary at the time, but both of these provide the medical team with basic but important information about you.

The rate at which patients are seen can vary significantly from day to day. There are occasions when outpatient staff are waiting for patients to arrive – the previous patient booked in may have cancelled. But on other occasions, consultations due to last ten minutes can unexpectedly take 45 minutes, perhaps because of a particularly complex case or a longer explanation of the treatment being needed. Most doctors are very keen not to rush people who may have been given complex or upsetting news, so a delay is not always a sign of the clinic not running smoothly. You should be told if there is an over-run, and should be given an estimated delay. Try to be patient and understanding if your appointment is delayed – in most instances it is simply taking more than the allotted time to give the patients before you the care that they need. We always suggest that people take something to read to make the time pass more quickly, because we are all too aware that sitting in a waiting room can be very dull if there is nothing to do! Here, a patient describes her experience of a long day in outpatients.

....

❝ *I had a lump in my breast which my GP wasn't sure about, so he referred me to the breast clinic at the local hospital. The appointment came through really quickly, within a few weeks, so I didn't have to wait too long. That was a relief, as I was worrying about it a bit. After seeing the doctor in the clinic I had to have an ultrasound of my breasts, a mammogram and a biopsy, and then wait to see the doctor again. The appointment was in the morning, but with all the waiting in-between these tests, I was there most of the day. I was glad I'd taken a book to read, but wished I'd also taken a packed lunch. I also wished I'd thought to wear a top and trousers, rather than a dress, which I had to take off for each examination. It was really good to get all the tests over with at once, though, and even better to find out that same day that the lump wasn't anything to worry about.* ❞

....

Who will see me in the clinic?

Most clinics are delivered under the leadership of a consultant, who you are likely to see on your first appointment even if only briefly. This is not guaranteed, however, and most consultants have a team of doctors and nurses working under their supervision (see Box 5).

Many people wish to see the consultant and you usually will if it is your first appointment in the clinic. However, some clinics will see more than 50 people in a session, so it is not possible for the consultant to see all of them. Junior doctors will discuss all the patients they see with a senior colleague and they will not make significant decisions about your care without doing so. They may also go and seek their advice during the consultation.

Box 5 *Examples of staff you may see in outpatient clinic*

- Consultant: the most senior doctor in the team, with specific expertise and experience in your condition
- Specialist registrar: a senior doctor who is in specialty training to become a consultant
- Staff grade doctor or associate specialist: a specialist doctor who is not on the specialty training path but who has experience of the clinical specialty concerned
- Core trainee or SHO (senior house officer): a junior doctor who as part of their early training is gaining experience in the specialty concerned
- Nurse consultant or clinical nurse specialist: a highly experienced nurse with in-depth training and experience in a specific area

---

You may also be seen by a specialist nurse or other healthcare professional in the clinic. These are usually very senior specialists who complement but do not replace the role of the doctor. Many are able to make clinical decisions themselves based on extra training and years of experience. For example, if you attend a rapid access chest pain clinic (because you have recently experienced chest pain), you may be seen by a specialist nurse who will decide which investigations to perform and whether you need to be started on any medication.

What happens when I see the doctor?

If it is your first visit, the doctor (or other healthcare professional) is likely to want a full medical history (see Chapter 11). They will ask about the reasons for your referral and about any other medical conditions that you have now or have had in the past. If you have a complex medical history, it is a good idea to write everything down beforehand to bring along with you (see Box 4). Outpatient clinic staff are always pleased when patients bring a list of their medicines with them, including the strengths, doses, and how many times a day they take each one.

The doctor will probably want to examine you. Any intimate examinations should include the offer of a chaperone, and if it is not offered you should ask for one if you wish. This will be another member of the healthcare team, often a healthcare assistant or more junior nurse, who will be there to reassure both you and the doctor. You are not obliged to be examined physically, but an examination will provide the doctor with much more information. If you think you may need to remove some of your clothing for an examination, you may want to wear something which is easy to take off and put on again. For example, female patients may prefer to wear separates rather than a dress, so that you can just remove part of your clothing.

Some patients prefer to be seen by a doctor of the same gender. Most frequently these are women, for religious or personal reasons, but men can and do have a preference too. Hospitals try their best to accommodate these requests, but it is sometimes just not possible – some clinics may only have male or female doctors. When this is the case the choice is a personal one, but we would reassure all patients that even intimate examinations are a very routine part of the job for specialist clinicians who may perform 15 or more such examinations a day.

Once the doctor has taken a history and examined you, they may suggest that you undergo some tests. These can include tests on blood and other bodily fluids, an ECG (to check your heart), X-rays, other radiological investigations or endoscopy. These and other investigations are described in Chapters 10–13. The doctor may also want to start you on a medication, or change the medication you are currently taking, or discuss the possibility of an operation.

Remembering everything that is said to you by the doctor can sometimes be difficult, particularly if you are worried or anxious, or if you are only just learning about your diagnosis. It is completely acceptable to ask the doctor to repeat anything they say or to explain it to you in another way. Ask them to write down key words and names of medication, or even draw you a diagram. Ask anything you need to – it is important that you understand, and clinicians are used to explaining things (see Box 6).

Box 6 *Questions to consider asking at your outpatient appointment*

- Why do I need these investigations?
- Why do I need to take medication and how long will I need it for?
- How often will I need to come to hospital?
- How will this illness affect my life?
- How will this illness affect my work?
- Where can I get more written information about my illness?
- Is there anyone else I can talk to about my illness?
- What happens next?

What happens after my appointment?

The doctor or nurse will write to your GP explaining what was said at your appointment and what happens next. They should ideally also send a copy of the letter to you. A few hospitals and clinicians do not yet do this routinely, or might ask you to sign a form before letters are copied to you. Asking for letters to be copied to you will help keep you informed, will help you to look things up afterwards, and – if you keep a file of the letters – will be helpful in ensuring all your information is available to whichever clinician sees you next.

The doctor may want to see you again in the outpatient clinic after you have had further investigations or after you have been started on a new medication. You may either make that next appointment there and then in the clinic, or you will be sent a letter with an appointment time after those investigations have been performed.

If you need to talk things through after your hospital appointment, arrange to visit your GP. Your hospital doctor and GP will communicate as much as is needed to make sure that you are getting the best possible care. Do not be afraid to keep asking questions – it is your health and you deserve honest answers and any support that you need.

CHAPTER FIVE

A planned admission

Planned admissions to hospital are known as 'elective admissions' because the patient chooses, or elects, to come into hospital either for the day or to stay longer. This could be for a variety of reasons, including to undergo an invasive procedure or operation, to receive medication that for some reason cannot be received at home, or to have a test which requires the patient to be in the hospital for a day or more.

In most cases, you will be asked to report to an admissions lounge or admissions unit. From there you will go to another ward or department for an investigation, operation or treatment. You may sometimes be asked to go straight to a specific ward, such as a renal ward if you have kidney disease, a haematology unit for blood disorders, or an oncology unit if you have a type of cancer. Admission to hospital does not always mean staying overnight (see Box 7). Many investigations and treatments can be carried out within a day, allowing you to return home that

---

Box 7 *Examples of investigations and treatments that may be carried out in one day*

- Administration of chemotherapy
- Blood transfusions and plasma exchanges
- Minor to moderate sized operations
- Angiography and stenting of blood vessels
- Endoscopy, including colonoscopy and bronchoscopy

evening. However, you will still be 'admitted' to hospital formally so that all proper checks can be carried out and to make an overnight stay easier if necessary. Hospitals are increasingly carrying out tests and treatments over the course of one relatively long day, and many more minor operations can now be carried out on a 'day

---

Box 8 *Admissions checklist*

Before admission

■ Check that you know:
  - the date and time you should arrive;
  - how you will get to the hospital;
  - where to report to at the hospital.
■ Check that you have made plans for:
  - the care of children, pets, or anyone else you look after;
  - any extra support you think you may need when you return home.
■ Check that you have packed:
  - your admission letter and any other information provided by the hospital;
  - the name and contact details of your GP;
  - a list of your usual medication and any allergies, and a small supply of your medication;
  - a list of any significant previous medical history;
  - magazines, music or books to keep you occupied;
  - your mobile phone and charger;
  - toiletries, underwear and perhaps a change of clothes (if you are likely to stay overnight).

On the day, before leaving home

■ Shower or bathe.
■ Follow any specific instructions you have been given, such as drinking plenty of water, taking medication, or not eating or drinking at all.

case' basis, without an overnight stay. This is partly because it is more efficient for the hospital but, more important, because patients avoid the disturbance and stress of staying overnight in hospital.

Preparing for an admission to hospital

When preparing for an elective admission, it is worth thinking about the questions below to allow you to prepare as well as possible. These points are also summarised in our admissions checklist in Box 8.

What time should I arrive?

This may be quite early in the morning. You may be asked to arrive from around 7am onwards, so make sure you plan your journey in advance and try to get a good night's sleep in your own bed before the early start. If you are at all uncertain, or the time is not stated clearly on your admission letter or appointment card, telephone to check the day before. It can be very frustrating to arrive much too early or, more important, too late.

What should I do in the days before my admission?

Make arrangements well in advance for the care of children, pets, or anyone else for whom you are a carer. Even if the admission is just for a day or overnight, you will probably be tired when you return home, so arrange any support you think you may need from friends and family, or from other sources such as social services or charities.

What should I do before leaving the house?

This is always a difficult question to answer, as it depends on the reason for going to hospital. We recommend showering or bathing that morning before you go to hospital. Washing with soap and water reduces the risk of carrying any unwanted bacteria on your skin into the hospital, which is good for both you and your fellow patients. You may not get an opportunity for a shower for a day or two after admission. There are baths and showers available in hospital, of course, but you may not be able to use them while you are recovering from an operation or procedure, and using your own is more comfortable for most of us. Depending on the reason for coming into hospital, you may also have specific instructions, such as drinking plenty of water or taking medication. Check any information that you have been given by the hospital, and if you are not sure, telephone the hospital to ask for more details in advance.

Can I eat and drink before admission?

If you are going to have an operation or certain other investigations, you may have been asked not to eat or drink for a certain period beforehand. You should not eat or drink anything for six hours before a general anaesthetic. In some cases the anaesthetist may allow you to drink water up to two hours before the operation, but if you are not sure it is best to err on the side of caution. You do not want to risk your operation or investigation being postponed.

What should I bring?

We recommend bringing things to keep you occupied, such as books, magazines, a small radio, or an MP3 player with headphones. Some people bring a laptop or tablet computer, allowing them to use the internet, watch videos and check their emails. You are responsible for the security of these devices unless they are formally locked away by hospital staff. Do bear in mind that there is often limited storage space and although some valuables can be safely locked away on the ward, it is easy to lose things if you are moving around the hospital. You do not want to be worrying about the safety of anything, such as jewellery, that is special to you or has significant sentimental value. If you are likely to be staying overnight, you will also need to bring toiletries, underwear and perhaps a change of clothes. More tips for what to bring are given in Chapter 18.

Can I make calls on my mobile?

The use of mobile telephones in hospital was controversial in the past, but mobiles are now usually permitted in most areas. Hospitals should have clear signs explaining areas where their use is permitted. You will generally not be allowed to use a mobile phone in or near an intensive care unit or a special care baby unit. When permitted, you can use your mobile phone to make calls or send text messages, but you should not use your telephone's camera to take photographs as this may compromise the confidentiality of your fellow patients. We believe that mobile telephones are generally good for patients, keeping lines of communication with family and friends open at a time when you may feel isolated or uncertain. Just occasionally, staff have to ask some patients to respect the privacy, dignity and safety of others when using them, so please do switch them off if you are asked to. Loud ring tones and alarms may also be confused with alarms being activated on medical monitoring equipment, and mobile signals may interfere with some equipment.

How can I help the staff provide the best treatment for me?

There are a number of things that you can do to help the staff and speed up the admission process:

- *Medication*. Do bring a list of your usual medicines with you; the hospital staff will not necessarily know what you usually take. You may also want to bring in a small supply. Any new ones will be supplied by the hospital, and the pharmacy will also be able to supply your usual medication if needed. However, if you bring in your own you will not have to wait for a supply to be sent to the ward and you can continue to use the brands with which you are familiar.

- *Communication between staff and your GP.* If possible, help by taking in the name and contact details of your GP. The hospital will usually have this already recorded, but it is always useful to check that their information is correct and up to date. Communication with your GP after your admission is vital, and anything you can do to make this process more efficient can be useful.
- *Additional information.* Some people have quite long and complex medical histories. (Your medical history consists of the illnesses, diagnoses, admissions and operations you have had previously.) Keeping a list of previous illnesses and treatments, with some details of when and where you were treated, can be very helpful for the doctors, nurses and other clinicians looking after you. Consider bringing copies of any records, investigations, letters and scan results to supplement the information already held by the hospital. Make sure you have your admission letter, which should give the name of the consultant looking after you and where you are to attend. Finally, any documentation with a hospital number or your central NHS number is useful.

How should I travel to the hospital?

This will very much depend on the hospital, whether there is car parking, and whether there are public transport options. We encourage you to come with someone else if possible. This friend or family member can provide both moral and practical support. Try to avoid driving yourself – you have enough to think about! Coming with someone else also means you do not have to leave your car at the hospital, which is desirable as hospital parking is now nearly always charged for, and can be very expensive for more than a few hours.

Where should I go when I arrive?

Your admission letter should provide clear information on where to go on arrival at the hospital. Hospitals generally have a number of different buildings, wings and levels. Often they have been built in a number of different stages. As a result, they can be difficult to navigate, even for the people who work in them. Hospitals often provide maps and instructions to help you, and there is usually additional information on their websites. Research this aspect of your visit; you may well be nervous on the day and anxious about finding the place to which you need to report. Consider a 'trial run' to find the ward or unit in question, especially if you have to attend the hospital in the weeks before your admission. If you have concerns, ask any member of staff, who will point you in the right direction and may even take you there. If all else fails, we suggest going to the reception desk in the main hospital entrance and asking for help.

The admission process

Once you have arrived at the hospital, the admission process begins. This will obviously vary depending on why you are being admitted, but there are some common steps.

Who will meet me there?

The most likely person to meet you when you arrive for an elective admission is a nurse. Alternatively, the receptionist or ward clerk, key members of the support staff who administer the unit in question, may be the first to meet you before you are seen by the nurses and doctors.

How will I be admitted?

Regardless of whether you are attending to have an investigation, such as an angiogram, or to have an operation or other treatment, you will require 'admitting'. The exact process will vary considerably depending on why you are being admitted. Broadly speaking, though, the nurse or another member of staff will check your name, date of birth, address and hospital number, and will record any important facts from your medical history.

Often, a basic set of observations will be done, to record your pulse, blood pressure, temperature, how quickly you are breathing and what the oxygen level is in your blood. You may also be asked to give a urine sample. You may be required to change into a hospital gown, and you may well be asked to wear a pair of special stockings to prevent blood clots forming in your legs (see Chapter 20). You will often meet a doctor from the team looking after you, who may take a medical history and examine you (see Chapter 11).

Why is there so much waiting?

It can be very frustrating being admitted to hospital. Often there can be quite a bit of sitting around and this can add to your anxiety. The staff looking after you should let you know why you are waiting. However, this sometimes does not happen, either because they are too busy, or because for them this is 'the norm' and from their point of view everything is running smoothly. Sometimes you have been asked to come early for good reason, even if your own procedure, investigation or operation might not be happening until later in the day. For example, there can be sudden changes to a series of operations because the first patient does not attend or another patient mistakenly ate something. If this happens, your operation or treatment may be brought forward. If you are uncertain why you are waiting, ask what is happening and when you will be transferred to your place of investigation or treatment. You may also want to clarify whether or not you are allowed to eat or drink in the meantime.

Will I move to different departments during my admission?

It is not uncommon for your 'journey' on the day of admission to finish in a different place to the one in which you started. For example, you might report to the admissions lounge, proceed to an operating theatre, then go to the recovery area, and then to a ward, before being moved to a discharge lounge before you travel home. Try to have this process mapped out for you before you start by asking the person who first admits you. It is particularly helpful for your relatives to know where they can visit you, and the best number to call if they wish to find out how you are. While this may seem complex, modern healthcare mostly tries to streamline the process. The plan is that you start where the investigation or treatment is and then move to a ward once this has been performed. Unfortunately, the nature of the NHS and the restricted number of beds mean that staff may not always know when your journey starts which ward you are going to finish on. If they do not, do not be alarmed; bed managers will be working behind the scenes to ensure that patients are discharged as quickly and as efficiently as possible so that bed space can be made available for you on the most appropriate ward.

This chapter has covered the very early stages of the process of being admitted to hospital. Later chapters describe the investigations, treatments and experiences you may have in hospital, whether you are there for a single day or for longer. Discharge from hospital at the end of your stay – after a day or two or after many months – is an important topic covered in Chapter 26.

CHAPTER SIX

An emergency admission

Sudden illness, regardless of its severity, is disturbing for anyone. Being admitted in an emergency, or even attending an emergency department with someone else, can be confusing and stressful. Patients can find that their diagnosis and management change on a minute-by-minute basis. Family members may struggle to find out exactly what is happening to their relative, because the staff are rightly focusing on assessing and treating them. We hope that understanding something of the way emergencies are treated and the way emergency departments work will at least make the process more comprehensible. This chapter explains what is likely to happen if you or a friend or relative are admitted as an emergency. We also highlight some questions that you or family members may want to ask, either after admission or if you are sent home.

The organisation of emergency services

Organising emergency medicine is difficult because the patients are so varied. Anyone may attend the emergency department at any time with any kind of illness. Staff see many people with minor injuries, but also have to cope with the sudden arrival of people who are very sick indeed. An ambulance crew may telephone the hospital to say that they have a patient on their way to hospital who is so ill that they will require, on arrival, an entire team of doctors, nurses and other clinical staff to be ready to focus on that one person. The patient's heart may have stopped and they may also have stopped breathing. These calls place significant demands on the department, so other less seriously ill patients may have to wait. Meanwhile, people are likely to be arriving continually with minor injuries and numerous other problems, asking to be seen by a doctor or specialist nurse. This can create considerable pressure on busy people in a stressful environment.

The general arrangements for emergency treatment are similar across the NHS. Major hospitals have specialised emergency departments, previously known as 'accident and emergency' or A&E. The individual requirements of different geographical areas mean that hospitals and their emergency facilities can vary. Increasingly, emergency services are concentrated in larger hospitals. The reasons for this are, first, that the departments themselves can be larger, with more staff and 24-hour presence of senior staff, and second, because they then have access to the full range of other hospital services.

Inside the emergency department there will be a waiting area and a reception desk where, if you are not seriously ill, you give your name and other basic information. After that you will be seen by a doctor or specialist nurse, as part of the 'triage' process (see below); they will make an initial assessment of how ill you are. You will then be taken to one of three areas inside the department, known as 'minors', 'majors' and 'resuscitation'. These are explained later and, as the names suggest, are designed for people with different kinds of problem.

In addition there may be other ward areas, with names such as 'rapid assessment units', 'medical assessment units' or 'acute assessment units'. These are for patients who have already seen their GP or a hospital doctor and have been sent for further observation or investigations. Some hospitals also have 'urgent care centres' for patients who arrive at the emergency department but really need to see a GP. Conditions for which this would be more appropriate include colds, coughs, sore ears, sore throats, most rashes and some minor injuries.

....

A patient has a cough, fever and some pains in his chest when he breathes in. He goes to see his GP, who assesses him and thinks he might be suffering from pneumonia. The GP tests the oxygen level in his blood and it is too low, so she sends the patient to the hospital. The GP's letter to the hospital asks them to confirm the diagnosis with blood tests and X-rays, and also to consider the need for admission for a few days to give oxygen and antibiotics. She sends this patient directly to the rapid assessment unit, rather than to the emergency department, because she feels confident that this is almost certainly a medical problem, and that the patient would benefit from being seen by the acute medical team.

....

How to obtain emergency treatment

Emergencies are by their very nature unplanned, and this unpredictability can make these admissions one of the most worrying reasons to visit a hospital. The list of conditions for which someone may attend a hospital as an emergency is almost limitless. There are many reasons for attending as an emergency patient and there are also a number of different routes to becoming an emergency patient. These are the five main ways in which you may go to the hospital as an emergency:

You decide to go to the emergency department yourself. You may simply feel very ill or very worried, for example having developed severe abdominal pain or shortness of breath, or with a suspected broken bone. Most of the patients in the emergency department have made their own decision to attend – or sometimes they have been advised to attend after telephoning the NHS helpline (currently 111 in England and Scotland).

You or another person may have called an ambulance. If you have to call an ambulance, try to give as much information as possible, clearly and concisely, about the problem and what it is you are worried about. If you have called an ambulance for someone else, you will have a few minutes to wait before it arrives. During this time, if possible, it can be helpful to get together any medicines that the person usually takes, the name and address of their GP, and any other important medical information. Do remember that ambulances are a precious resource to be called when someone needs immediate medical attention and rapid transport to a hospital; they are not a taxi service to the hospital. However, if you are seriously worried about yourself or a family member, do not hesitate to ring 999 immediately. Frequently, the ambulance crew may start basic early diagnosis and treatment when they arrive, and may relay information to the hospital if they feel the situation is critical and requires doctors and nurses to be waiting on arrival there.

You have seen your GP at their surgery or in your home. Your GP may assess your symptoms and decide that you require a consultation with a specialist doctor immediately. If this happens, they will telephone the relevant hospital team directly. You will then be asked to go to the hospital, and be told to attend either the emergency department or another specialist unit.

You may contact your specialist team directly. This only applies to patients with chronic conditions. For instance, patients with chronic kidney disease may have the contact details of a member of the team – such as a specialist nurse – or of a 'rapid access unit' or helpline. These arrangements are relatively new, many having been established within the last decade to improve the access of patients with chronic conditions to specialist help. If you suffer a decline in your condition, you may call the team and be told to come to hospital for further assessment. Generally in these circumstances you would go directly to the specialist ward or admitting unit, but you may be told to attend the emergency department and be admitted there.

You may be admitted direct from the outpatient department. If the doctor seeing you in an outpatient clinic feels that you need immediate investigations or treatment, they can arrange then and there for you to be admitted. You may go directly to one of the wards, or via an assessment unit within the emergency department where investigations and treatment can be given while you are waiting for a hospital bed.

Attending as an emergency patient

Although the exact process varies according to the severity of their illness, most patients follow a fairly standard pathway when they attend as an emergency. First, patients are booked in (or 'registered'), a mainly administrative process in which the patient (or the person accompanying them if they are too ill) provides basic information, such as their name, date of birth, address and GP's name and address.

Next, patients are 'triaged'. Triage is an essential function in the emergency department, where many patients with very different problems can arrive simultaneously. Its purpose is to ensure that patients are treated in the order of their clinical urgency. Urgency is not the same as severity, but refers to the need for time-critical intervention. People who are seriously ill almost always need urgent treatment, but some less serious conditions also need rapid intervention. Triage is usually carried out by specialised nurses or by doctors. The triage assessment generally takes no more than five minutes, aiming to balance speed and thoroughness; it is not about making a diagnosis, but about assessing the likely severity and urgency of the condition. During triage, patients have to be grouped very quickly into people who need help but who are not seriously ill, those whose condition is more serious, and a small number whose life is hanging in the balance. When people attend an emergency department, they are not simply placed in a queue of people to be seen as you might be in a shop. If they are very sick, they will jump to first place in the queue and be seen immediately. Conversely, if someone has sprained their ankle, they may have to wait while other critically ill people are seen first.

In the majority of cases, patients are well enough to register themselves and speak to the triage nurse before being seen by a doctor. After triage the patient is sent to the most appropriate assessment and treatment area. In the most urgent categories, patients will be seen immediately or within a few minutes, and assessment and treatment are expected to occur at the same time. In less urgent cases, patients may wait for a while before seeing the next available doctor or nurse specialist.

The first task for most doctors seeing a new patient is to make a diagnosis and consider what treatment is needed. However, the emergency department nurse or doctor also has to consider two more urgent questions, even when they do not know exactly what is wrong with the patient. First, how serious is this problem? And second, does this patient need to be admitted to hospital? A good example would be abdominal pain; this has many different causes, some of which are serious and some of which are not. Often the doctor is not able to be sure what the precise cause of the problem is. However, by combining training, experience and initial results of investigations, a doctor can be fairly confident about whether or not the symptoms point to a serious condition that requires urgent treatment even if the exact diagnosis is uncertain. If the condition does not seem serious, the patient may be allowed home without a diagnosis or any treatment beyond painkillers but with specific instructions to watch for particular signs and return if necessary.

The emergency department

After triage, a patient is taken to one of a number of different areas of the emergency department. Where they are taken depends on the urgency and severity of their illness.

Minors

Patients who are walking and have relatively localised, specific problems are taken to 'minors'. These problems are often the result of accidents, and include sprained ankles, cuts, skin infections and 'foreign bodies' (such as a piece of glass inside a wound). Most patients with these problems will not require admission to hospital for an overnight stay, although they may be asked to see their GP in the next few days for a further check-up. Alternatively, they may be asked to return to hospital to see either the emergency department doctors again, or another team – for example, the orthopaedic and trauma surgeons in the fracture clinic.

Majors

Patients are placed in 'majors' if they are considered too unwell or potentially unwell to sit in the waiting area or in 'minors'. They may or may not be seriously ill, but their symptoms certainly need further investigation. For instance, patients presenting with chest pain, abdominal pain, shortness of breath or uncontrolled bleeding will find themselves in 'majors'. They will be monitored frequently and have blood tests, urine tests and radiological investigations such as X-rays. Most of these patients will be admitted to stay in hospital overnight, although some may be discharged home. For instance, a patient with chest pain may go on to have tests which show them to be healthy; the chest pain was due to indigestion and they can go home with some new medication.

Resuscitation

Patients whose lives are considered to be in immediate danger or who require continuous monitoring and high levels of nursing care are placed in the 'resuscitation' area. They are usually taken there straight from the ambulance arrival bay, and very often the crew will have telephoned ahead requesting that the patient is met by a team of doctors, nurses and other staff. Patients requiring resuscitation might, for instance, have been in a serious car accident or have suffered a severe heart attack. If a patient attends with friends, colleagues or relatives, these people may be asked to wait in the relatives' room and help with registering the patient while the clinical team get to work resuscitating the patient. Investigations (see Chapters 10–13) can be organised and performed in a very short period of time, to help make the right diagnosis and allow treatment to start as soon as possible.

A patient in this situation is likely to be too unwell to participate actively in their own care, beyond trying to co-operate and communicate as well as possible. Relatives and friends can be invaluable sources of information for the staff, and someone should be sent to talk to them as soon as possible to provide important information regarding their loved one.

The doctors may take a 'SAMPLE' history from either the patient or accompanying relatives and friends, focusing on the following six points:

- **S**igns and Symptoms that the patient was suffering in the preceding moments
- **A**llergies to any medicines or other substances
- **M**edication that the patient currently takes
- **P**ast medical history
- **L**ast time of any food or drink (which can be very important if the patient requires an immediate anaesthetic)
- **E**vents leading up to the injury and/or illness

Almost all patients brought to the resuscitation area of the emergency department will be admitted to one of the high dependency or intensive care settings in the hospital (see Chapter 9). Relatives should ask for a telephone number or a named ward that they can contact later. If the staff are unsure where the patient will be sent, they should contact the emergency department or the main hospital number the next day to find out – staff will have a record of where the patient was sent.

Once a patient has attended as an emergency patient and been assessed by the doctors, there are three main options. First, they may be sent home and recover as anticipated. Second, they may be sent home but then find that they do not get better or even that their condition deteriorates. Third, they may be admitted to hospital. We will consider these in turn in terms of what the patient or a relative might need to do or ask.

What do I need to ask if I am told I can go home?

Being told that you can go home is obviously good news, but there are a few questions you should ask before you leave hospital.

What do you think is wrong with me?

If the doctors have made a specific diagnosis which identifies the reasons for your symptoms, make sure you know what it is and what the implications are. Sometimes the doctors will have assessed the severity of your symptoms but not made a formal diagnosis; however, they will have ruled out serious conditions and be confident that you are not seriously ill. For instance, people sometimes get aches and pains which are never fully explained. In this case, however, ask what you should do if the problem continues or gets worse.

Do I need to take any new medication?

If so, what do you need to take and for how long? Common new medicines include a course of painkillers, antibiotics, anti-inflammatories, laxatives, antacids, or medicines to put on your skin such as creams. Make sure you know what you have been prescribed, how long the medication should be continued for, and how to get further supplies if needed. This is especially important if you have been told to take the medication for more than a few days.

Will you contact my GP or do you want me to inform them?

Normally GPs are sent all the details of emergency attendances, but sometimes you may be given a letter to drop into your GP's surgery or put in the post.

Will I have any further investigations?

You may be asked to return for a further assessment. For example, people with possible fractures of the bones in their hands or wrists will be asked to return for a follow-up appointment to assess their progress. If you are asked to come back, make sure you know where you need to come to and write down the date and time.

What was the name of the doctor who looked after me in the emergency department?

This is useful if you need to come back, or have a query later on.

What do I do if I am sent home and my symptoms get worse?

Sometimes in the early stages of a condition, doctors may not be completely sure what is wrong with you. Illnesses show themselves in different ways in different people and it can often be difficult to be sure of the diagnosis at the first assessment. In these circumstances, you may be allowed home 'conditionally'. This means that, while you are well enough to go home, you must watch carefully for any 'red-flag' signs or symptoms of deterioration that require you to return to hospital for further investigations and treatment. There is no need to be anxious about being sent home, but make sure you know what these red flag symptoms are and what to do if you notice them.

....

A patient injures her head and comes to the emergency department to check whether she has done any lasting damage. A few key points in the history and examination allow the doctor to conclude that it is probably only a bump, with no long-term consequences. However, the doctor knows that a very small percentage (less than 1%) of people who injure their head have some bleeding in the head afterwards which cannot be detected immediately. The hospital obviously cannot admit everyone with a knock on the head, as the hospital beds would quickly become full of people who are healthy and very fed up! Instead, doctors give all those for whom they have a very low level of concern some clear instructions: the patient must stay with someone who can keep an eye on them and watch for a list of signs or symptoms which require immediate return to the hospital (such as vomiting, unremitting headaches or visual disturbance).

....

What do I need to consider if I am admitted to hospital?

Emergency admissions are by their very nature 'out-of-the-blue' and worrying. The questions and explanations below are aimed at helping you and/or your family and friends to cope with this difficult situation.

Where am I going and which team will look after me?

Odd as it may seem, the doctors in the emergency department do not admit patients themselves into the main hospital. Instead, they will refer you to another team of hospital doctors who are 'on-call' for emergency admissions. The team you are referred to will depend on your diagnosis, but nearly all hospitals with an emergency department will have specialist teams who come to the emergency department. These include orthopaedic and trauma surgeons, the physicians (or 'medics'), the general surgeons, and the obstetrics and gynaecology team. Sometimes you may have to be moved again later, to the care of a more specialist team. A good example of this might be urological ('waterworks') emergencies, for which patients may be admitted at night or over the weekend by the general surgeons and then later 'handed-over' to the urologists in normal working hours. You should always ask which team is looking after you as this is something helpful for all patients and relatives to know. Clinical staff talk about a patient being 'under the care of' or even just 'under' a specific team. If you have been in hospital before for the same condition, you may well know which team will be caring for you after admission.

What do you think is wrong with me?

The medical term for this is 'provisional diagnosis', which is essentially the best assessment that can be made without further investigations; the exact diagnosis is not always clear at first. However, a list of possible diagnoses, or conditions that the doctors are seeking to rule in or rule out, should be explained to you. The provisional diagnosis and immediate management plan should be explained to all patients and/or their carers at the point of admission to the hospital.

Which ward am I going to?

Ideally, you will be admitted to a specialist ward relevant to your diagnosis. For instance, if you have fallen over and broken your hip you will be admitted to the trauma ward. Sometimes a bed is not available and so you are given a bed on a different ward until a bed in a more appropriate ward is available. This is not ideal as the nurses on each ward tend to specialise in that specific area, but it should not be a concern as long as it does not last too long. Ask when a bed will become available and what provisions are being put in place to make sure your care does not suffer. Other factors can determine which ward you will be placed in; for example, if you are suspected of suffering from an infectious disease, a single room is more important than which particular ward you are on.

But I've got nothing with me!

Patients who are admitted as an emergency are likely to be ill-prepared, without any clothes, personal toiletries, money or reading materials. Most wards in the hospital that look after emergency patients will have spare supplies such as toothbrushes, toothpaste, soap, shampoo and hospital gowns or pyjamas. These are not usually of the highest quality, so it is much better if relatives or friends can bring your own things in for you. If no one is available to bring your own clothes and toiletries, you can often use the hospital shop, sometimes run by the Friends of the Hospital, which will stock basic supplies. The shop is usually located in the main entrance of the hospital, by reception. If you cannot get out of bed, have a friendly word with a medical student, student nurse or healthcare assistant and you may be able to find yourself a courier! Finally, a trolley service is common in most hospitals and most wards, so ask the nurses when the trolley service is due to come round if you cannot find anyone to go to the shop for you. We give more suggestions about looking after yourself in Chapter 18.

Why am I moving wards?

As the diagnosis becomes clear, as your needs change or as a bed becomes available, you may move ward again or even be looked after by a new team. Do not be disturbed by this, but do ask why it is happening. The usual reason is that the new team will provide more appropriate care for the next phase of your recovery. However, moving patients round the hospital should only be done when absolutely necessary, and most hospitals keep this to a minimum wherever possible.

How soon can I go home?

As soon as you feel better and think you might be better off at home, you should ask about plans for your discharge from hospital. 'Discharge' is a formal process of ending your stay in hospital and supporting you either to go home or to be looked after somewhere else (see Chapter 26). Your doctors and nurses will also be thinking, from very early on, about how long you might be in hospital, and should share this information with you. Ask them about going home as soon as you feel ready to do so. This will give you something to look forward to and also allow your friends, relatives and carers to plan your return home.

Being in
hospital

CHAPTER SEVEN

The people who look after you

Hospitals employ huge numbers of staff – the NHS is the UK's largest employer, and one of the five largest employers in the world. While in or visiting hospital, you will come across a wide range of healthcare professionals and staff, with different roles, grades, titles and uniforms. This chapter explains who some of these people are, and their roles and responsibilities, and suggests who to ask for help and advice (see Figure 1).

Figure 1 Who will look after me?

Doctors

When you are admitted to hospital, you will be under the care of a designated medical or surgical team, which will include a number of doctors at different stages of their training. The specific team and the ward chosen for you will be guided by the type of problem you have. In some settings, all the patients on a particular ward will be looked after by the same medical team. In other cases, teams look after patients with a particular illness or condition who might be distributed across a number of different wards. Even if all the patients on your ward are not looked after by the same team, they will usually have similar problems, such as fractures, heart problems or liver disease. The skills needed by the medical, nursing and other clinical staff vary by clinical specialty, so it is helpful for wards to specialise in this way.

You should expect to be seen every day by at least one of the doctors in your team for a review of your progress and symptoms, so that decisions can be made regarding your care and plans can be made for discharge. Broadly speaking, there are three tiers of doctors: consultants, middle-grade doctors (often referred to as 'registrars') and junior doctors.

Consultants

The consultant is the most senior doctor and the person who has ultimate responsibility for your care. You should expect to be seen by a consultant within 24 hours of your admission. The frequency with which you will see them after this varies significantly between hospitals, specialties and individual consultants. Consultants often have many patients, who may be on different sites, and they also take on other responsibilities in the hospital. If you are seriously ill or recovering from a major operation, your consultant will be reviewing your care every day either in person or through discussion with other senior members of the team.

Middle-grade doctors or 'registrars'

These doctors have completed their medical school training and have at least four years additional full-time clinical experience. In the vast majority of cases, they are responsible for the day-to-day running of the medical team. You will see the registrar looking after you on a daily or near-daily basis; they will make most of the decisions about your care (with the oversight and support of their consultants), and will supervise the junior doctors. As with any job, there is variation in their seniority and thus the amount of supervision and input they will require from their consultant. The most experienced will be within a few months of starting their own consultant job, and will be near-autonomous individuals requiring very little oversight and guidance. Others may be in their first year as a registrar and will require more support; they may seek help and clarity on their decisions from their consultant more frequently. Do not be afraid to ask a registrar questions about this, and about whether or not they have spoken to the consultant that day about your care.

There are a number of different job titles that you may hear people use at this level, which can be potentially confusing. There are two reasons for this. The first is that reforms of medical training in 2008 changed the name of doctors in advanced training from 'specialist registrar' to 'specialty registrar', but the older term is still frequently used. The second is that not all those working at this level are on training programmes; some are working at this level in permanent or 'fixed-term' posts. These staff grades or associate specialists work as middle-grade doctors and may also be referred to as 'registrars'. You may hear all these terms used, but essentially they are just different names for doctors who are specialising in a particular area of medicine or surgery but have not yet become consultants.

Junior doctors

After leaving medical school, newly qualified doctors have to complete two years on a Foundation training programme. Depending on their area of medicine, most then work for two or three more years as 'core trainees' before progressing to be a registrar in their chosen area. So Foundation year doctors (FY1s and FY2s) have just graduated from medical school and are in the first two years of their postgraduate training. They spend the majority of their time on the wards, where they perform a lot of the vital day-to-day administrative and clerical work; this includes prescribing medication, requesting investigations, liaising with other teams or healthcare staff, and documenting proceedings. They are the doctors most commonly called by the nursing staff for initial medical assessment and advice if they are concerned about a patient. In this two-year period Foundation year doctors work in a number of different medical and surgical specialties to gain some broad experience that will act as a practical 'foundation' for the rest of their careers. The UK's General Medical Council describes this period as 'a bridge between medical school and specialist or general practice training'. Junior doctors rotate through different placements every three to six months, and different programmes will have slightly different 'flavours' to allow some choice and to appeal to different junior doctors depending on what they want to do in the long term.

Core trainees (CT1s, CT2s and CT3s) have completed their foundation year training and are gaining more experience within their chosen specialist fields before applying to become registrars. They will often support and supervise their more junior colleagues while they acquire important knowledge, skills and experience that will allow them to progress.

Despite a decade of Foundation training and Core training, you may hear junior doctors referred to as 'house officers' and 'senior house officers' (or SHOs). Doctors in their first foundation year are now generally known as 'FY1s', but before 2005 doctors in their first year out of medical school were called 'pre-registration house officers'. Old habits die hard, particularly in a traditional culture such as medicine.

Medical students

Most hospitals have a strong focus on education and training, and some are specifically designated as 'teaching' or 'university' hospitals. In these, you are likely to see medical students attached to a team of doctors. This is an important part of their training, which helps them to gain knowledge and experience. You may be asked if you would be happy for medical students to ask you questions or examine you. Sharing your experience with them allows them to practise both their history-taking and their examination techniques. If you would prefer not to be questioned or examined by a medical student, you can refuse, but please remember that even the most eminent professors started off as students!

Medical students, and indeed all clinical students, are professionals in training and have the same professional obligations as their senior counterparts. They should speak to you respectfully and maintain your confidentiality. The vast majority will be polite, inquisitive and kind. Students often have a lot more time than doctors to talk to you and to accompany you for investigations or procedures. However, if you have any concerns about the medical students on the team, we advise you to speak to the registrar.

Nurses

Each ward is staffed by a nursing team which looks after all the patients on that ward. There will always be nurses available to care for, support and reassure you, and to help you with problems. There are a number of different types and grades of nurse. We cannot describe all the different types in different specialties, but it is helpful to know the main grades and responsibilities.

Matrons and clinical nurse managers

Matrons and clinical nurse managers are senior people in the hospital who are in overall charge of nursing in your area. These nurses are often responsible for a whole department or a number of wards (for example, all medical wards or all emergency areas) and will therefore be overseeing all the nursing within that department. Because they have such wide responsibilities, they are unlikely to be based on any one particular ward and you may not see them during your stay.

Sister/Charge nurse

The sister (female) or charge nurse (male) is the nurse who is responsible for the overall day-to-day running of a whole ward. They may also be referred to as the ward manager or the nurse-in-charge, as they are in charge of all the other nurses on the ward. You will see them on the ward, but although they will be involved in some direct patient care, they may not actually look after you as they are also overseeing all the other nurses and the safe and efficient running of the ward. If you ever have any serious concerns about your care, talking to the sister or charge nurse is the first step in addressing them.

Staff nurses

Staff nurses are usually the most numerous common grade of nurse on the ward. They are responsible for the day-to-day care of a group of patients; for example, all the patients in a particular bay. They should be able to answer questions about what is happening, and are most likely to be your first point of contact with any questions. Senior staff nurses will be carrying out many of the same tasks as the staff nurses, but are more experienced. They are often the nurse in charge of a particular ward or area during a shift.

Healthcare assistants (HCAs)

As well as qualified nurses, your ward is likely to employ health-care assistants (HCAs). HCAs have basic healthcare training, but not a nursing qualification. They are employed to assist with direct patient care. They may help you with your personal care

(washing, dressing and toileting), and with your eating and drinking, and may also help the nursing team with more specialised
tasks like recording your 'observations' or 'vital signs' (such as
temperature, pulse and blood pressure).

Student nurses

First-hand experience of caring for patients is an essential part
of nurse training. Your ward nursing team may include student
nurses who are doing practical training. They are likely to have
similar duties to the HCAs, and will help the trained nurses.

Clinical nurse specialists (CNSs)

There may also be a specialist nurse as part of the team looking
after your care. CNSs are experienced nurses who have chosen to
specialise in a particular field. Examples include stoma nurses in
gastrointestinal surgery, who care for and educate patients with
stomas (surgically created openings on the abdomen which allow
faeces or urine to exit the body into a special bag rather than the
usual way), or CNSs in diabetes, who help with the management
of patients with diabetes. Unlike the other nurses, who are ward-
based, these nurses are more often attached to a medical team.
They work across wards and specialties, complementing the roles
of the doctors, and they often provide education to other staff,
including doctors.

There is no national standard for nursing uniforms and you are
likely to find that the colour and pattern or type of uniform worn
by each type of nurse will vary among hospitals. However, within
each hospital the same uniform will be worn by each grade of
nurse and this will be the same for all the wards within that hospital. For example, all the staff nurses will be wearing the same
uniform, which will be different from the one that all the HCAs
are dressed in.

Other healthcare professionals

There are many other members of the hospital team, some or all of whom will be involved in your care.

Pharmacists

Pharmacists visit the wards most days and assess prescriptions to make sure that they are safe and appropriate. They also advise doctors on prescribing, and nurses on drug administration. Pharmacists will check that the medication that you normally take is being prescribed correctly now that you are in hospital, and will ensure that the ward has supplies of any medicines that you need. They will be able to answer questions about your medicines. When you are ready to go home, they will prepare a supply of medication for you to take home with you, and make sure that you and your GP are provided with information about any medicines that were changed while you were in hospital.

Physiotherapists

Physiotherapists help people affected by injury, illness or disability through movement and exercise, manual therapy, education and advice. They work in almost all areas of a hospital, from the outpatient setting to intensive care. Their roles can vary widely. Some physiotherapists work in outpatients, helping relatively well people rehabilitate after joint surgery or trauma, while others specialise in treating very sick patients in intensive care or supporting recovery after a major stroke. They assess your movement and physical abilities and guide you in your recovery with physical exercises and rehabilitation. They may need to ask questions about your home and your usual day-to-day activities in order to understand what level of movement and function you usually have. Relatives, carers or friends can also be a useful source of information for physiotherapists to understand your abilities and to develop individual goals for your recovery. Before discharge, physiotherapists may be asked to assess your strength and mobility as well as your ability to walk, climb stairs and perform the movements you will require to look after yourself when you are outside hospital.

Occupational therapists

Like physiotherapists, occupational therapists work with patients to support their return to ordinary life after a period of illness. However, they consider all types of problems of day-to-day living, including your emotional state. Some occupational therapists specialise in working with people with mental illness or learning disabilities. An occupational therapist will help you restore lost skills, build confidence, and solve the practical problems you may have in carrying out everyday activities due to your illness. They may offer modifications to your home, such as additional handrails, or special equipment to assist with daily activities. They are part of a team of people who ensure you will be safe in your own home when you are discharged. They may accompany you home to assess you in your own environment and identify any adaptations that may be required.

Dieticians

Dieticians provide expertise in diet and nutrition. They see patients who are considered to need extra support with their diet, and they may develop individual eating plans or dietary modifications. Your diet can be affected for a number of reasons when you are unwell; you may suffer a loss of appetite, be unable to eat certain types of food, or need more calories or certain vital vitamins, elements or salts. Dieticians are particularly important in units caring for patients who might not be able to eat or digest their food in a normal manner, such as gastrointestinal surgery units. Here, some patients may receive additional nutrition directly into parts of their intestines using tubes placed through their nose or abdominal wall ('enteral nutrition'). Others may not be able to use their gastrointestinal tract at all, and they are placed on 'parenteral nutrition'. This is where a specially formulated liquid of protein, fats and sugars is transfused directly through a special feeding cannula into a large vein.

Speech and language therapists

Speech and language therapists assess and treat people with speech, language and communication problems to enable them to communicate to the best of their ability. In addition, they use their knowledge of the voice box and throat to help assess, investigate and treat patients who are having swallowing difficulties.

Non-clinical staff

As well as the various healthcare professionals described above, you will meet many other groups of staff. These include porters, who are responsible for transporting patients and equipment around the hospital, and ward receptionists or 'ward clerks', who manage the day-to-day administration of the ward such as keeping the hospital information system up to date. These administrative and support staff do not have clinical responsibilities, but they can help you in many other ways. For instance, the ward receptionist is a key member of the team and is often a useful source of information about the ward and the hospital.

The chaplaincy or faith service

Most hospitals have a faith team or service, sometimes referred to as the chaplaincy. In our increasingly diverse culture, more and more faiths are catered for. Even if there is not a full-time member of the clergy from your faith attached to the hospital, the service will have links with local faith organisations and places of worship. The ward staff will be able to put you in touch with a priest or equivalent on request. There will normally be some-one available around the clock to tend to the spiritual needs of patients, families and loved ones.

Volunteers

Most hospitals have active volunteer services, whose volunteers may guide people around the hospital, run a shop or café, and provide a trolley service to the ward which carries newspapers, books and confectionery. Volunteers often play a key role within the chaplaincy service too, and sometimes provide an advocacy service; this gives support, company and help to patients who do not have friends and family to support them during their time in hospital. The advocacy service can be used for something as straightforward as having another person with you during an outpatient appointment. Ask ward staff or volunteers themselves about their roles if you see them. Most volunteers have previ-ously been patients, so you may also want to consider this role for yourself!

CHAPTER EIGHT

The hospital ward

Whether your admission to hospital is planned or unplanned, you will become an 'inpatient' on a ward. The ward may seem a little strange and unfamiliar, particularly if it is your first time in hospital. This chapter will help you understand how a typical ward works and what will happen while you are there, and will provide you with some information about the daily routine. Later in this book, Chapter 18 gives more information that complements the information below. We start by describing some of the different types of hospital wards.

Types of hospital ward

While most wards look similar and are arranged in a relatively standard fashion, they have different purposes and may care for very different kinds of patients.

Acute or short stay wards

The majority of patients in these wards will have been admitted as an emergency, either directly or via the emergency department (ED). These patients often have a wide variety of symptoms and may not yet have a definite diagnosis. During their time on this ward they may be receiving urgent treatment while also having investigations and seeing doctors from different specialties to establish a diagnosis and plan future treatment. Confusingly, these wards are known by different names in different hospitals. A few common titles are the medical assessment (or admissions) unit (MAU), the emergency assessment unit (EAU) or the acute medical/surgical unit (AM/SU). Patients usually only stay on these wards for a short time (from a few hours up to a day or two) before being sent home or transferred to another ward in the hospital that specialises in their particular problem.

Specialist wards

There are many different types of specialist wards and we cannot list them all here. If you have a heart problem, you will almost always find yourself admitted to a cardiology ward. If, however, you require continuous cardiac monitoring, this may be on a coronary care unit (CCU); the CCU may be a section of the cardiology ward or may be a separate unit, depending on the hospital. Alternatively, if you have a broken bone and require surgery, you will be taken to a ward specialising in trauma and orthopaedics. If you are admitted with kidney failure, you will be admitted to the renal unit. Other medical and surgical specialties will also have their own specific wards. While these wards may all look very similar, the nurses, doctors and therapists based on each will have a specific interest and expertise in the relevant conditions, and specialised equipment will be available. For example, the renal unit will have dialysis machines, but the cardiology ward will not.

Care of the elderly wards

Elderly patients (usually classed as people over the age of 75, but this varies from hospital to hospital) often have complex sets of needs and may be cared for on a specialist ward. Patients on these wards frequently have a number of different medical conditions at the same time, and will be managed by specialists in the care of elderly people. The wards place a strong emphasis on rehabilitation and the regaining of independence. Occupational therapy and physiotherapy are a very important part of the

overall treatment programme. Note that you will not necessarily
be on such a ward just because you are over 75; if you have
one main condition requiring treatment by a specialist team – an
operation, for example – you will be looked after on the appropriate surgical ward.

High dependency units (HDUs)

Some patients are critically unwell and need a much higher
level of care. People who are very sick will be cared for in an
intensive care unit (ICU), described in the next chapter. HDUs are
for patients who need constant monitoring and higher levels of
nursing support, but do not need the full intensive care environment. Staff on HDU wards are highly trained and experienced
in the care of people who are very ill. The HDU provides more
nurses per patient (usually one nurse to two or three patients),
as well as more specialist equipment which is not available on
general wards.

Rehabilitation units

These units are generally located in the community, but may
also be found in hospitals. They are for patients who no longer
require medical treatment from specialist doctors, but still require
nursing and other therapies daily to allow them to continue to
improve. You may be transferred here from a specialist ward after
your initial medical treatment is complete. The aim is often, but
not always, to support patients in their recovery to the point that
they can manage in their own home. Units like these often focus
on a particular area, such as spinal injury rehabilitation or stroke
rehabilitation.

General information about hospital wards

The organisation of care on the wards varies between hospitals,
but the day-to-day routine is generally fairly similar.

Where will I sleep?

Wards are usually organised into areas known as 'bays', each of which typically has four to six beds. Even if the whole ward is mixed in terms of gender, each bay will be for men or for women. You will have your own separate area within the bay, which can be screened off by a curtain. Your area (sometimes called a cubicle) will typically have a bed, a chair, a table which can fit over the bed, and a bedside cabinet (which may be or may not be lockable). There is room to keep a few personal possessions, but try to avoid bringing in anything of great sentimental or financial value. A nurse will ask you if you want anything to be locked away safely. If any of your property is to be kept by the ward staff, it will be documented to ensure that everything is accounted for when you leave.

Can I have my own room?

Single rooms, often known as 'side rooms', are mainly reserved for patients whose conditions may be infectious to other patients or who are very susceptible to infection from others. If you feel that you need a side room, you can discuss this with the team in charge of your care. However, side rooms are limited in number and the team may not be able to accommodate such requests unless you need one for medical reasons. If the option is not available but a single room is very important to you, ask if there is a private ward in the hospital that you could be transferred to. These wards are nearly always single-room occupancy, but of course you would need to pay, either with your own money or through private healthcare insurance.

Toilets and showers

Toilets and shower facilities are usually shared with other patients and will again be single gender. You will be shown where they are located when you are admitted. Basic soap and towels will be available, but you can make yourself more comfortable by bringing in your own towels and toiletries (see Chapter 18). If you are unable to reach the toilet and washing facilities, the nursing staff will help you with washing, and will bring bed pans or commodes to your bedside.

Calling a nurse or doctor

At every bedside there will be a buzzer to press if you need help. Nurses can also be found at the nurses' station, a reception-like area usually centrally located in the ward. If you or a member of your family need to speak to a doctor, it will generally be easiest to ask the nurses to contact them for you, although you will regularly see more junior members of the medical team on the ward.

Cleanliness

Wards should have a very high standard of cleanliness, and in the authors' experience this standard is increasingly met. The years of dirty, unclean wards now seem, except in very rare cases, to be behind us. You will regularly see cleaners on the wards and they may start very early in the morning. If you have any concerns with the level of cleanliness or hygiene on the ward, you should definitely tell the nurse in charge of the ward. You should see dispensers of alcohol gel at the end of every bed, in the corridors, and at the entrances and exits to wards. Regularly cleaning your hands with alcohol gel helps control infections and protects both you and other patients. All staff, patients and visitors should use the gel regularly. Chapter 19 provides more information on hand hygiene and prevention of infection.

The daily routine

Life on the ward can feel hectic; there is a lot to do, the days are long, and many different people are coming and going. Days start early and the hustle and bustle can be disorientating, but after a couple of days the pattern of activity will become more familiar.

The nursing rounds

Your day is likely to start with the arrival of the new shift of nursing staff. When nurses on the day shift arrive to take over from those on the night shift, they do a handover round in which they bring the new team up to date on each patient's condition. This may start as a team meeting in a room on the ward, but the nursing team will usually then go around the ward patient by patient so that the night staff can communicate any important events or changes that have occurred overnight. The nursing staff will also perform a set of observations on each patient (pulse, blood pressure, temperature, etc.) first thing in the morning, and there will be a drug administration round. These tasks may be done by the night staff just before handover, or by the new day team arriving. The nursing staff and healthcare assistants will also help patients get up, get washed and get dressed. They will change and refresh bedding and linen. All this may happen before, during or after breakfast has been served! Some patients will also need regular blood tests to monitor their progress, although in most cases taking blood samples for testing is now performed by phlebotomists (specially trained blood-takers) rather than by doctors or nurses.

When will I see a doctor?

Doctors' ward rounds typically start between 7am and 9am and can take several hours to complete. It is therefore difficult to predict when you will be seen. You should expect to be seen by a member of the medical team at least once a day to review your progress and adjust your treatment if necessary. The morning ward rounds can be very quick and business-like. This is often due to necessity; the surgeons, for instance, may need to be in the operating theatre from 8.15am, so are trying to see all their patients between 7.30am and the start of their operating list.

If there are any particular questions you want to ask, it is helpful to write them down beforehand so you can focus on what it is you want to know from the doctors. If you feel you need a more in-depth discussion, it might be better to request a meeting or to ask for the doctors to return later in the day. This will ensure that you get the time you need.

Tests, investigations and medication

The early part of your stay in hospital may be quite busy. You will find that your day will be interspersed with further observations, medication and visits to different departments for tests or treatments. Observations of your vital signs or the administration of medication may also be carried out at night, but this will only be done when it is necessary for your care. Where possible, patients are left undisturbed between about 10pm and 6am. Wards can be noisy places, with many beeps and buzzers and constant activity, so you may find it useful to bring some ear plugs and an eye mask to help you sleep (see Chapter 18).

Once you have had the main investigations, you often have to wait for results and it can seem that nothing is happening. Behind the scenes, your team are likely to be reviewing your progress carefully and planning next steps. Many tests and investigations take time and it can be frustrating to wait for results. If you are worried by the time it is taking, or think you may be well enough to be at home, ask your team about your progress, what is likely to happen next and whether you still need to be in hospital at this point. Both doctors and nurses should be able to help you with your questions – or at least give you an indication of when your questions can be answered and by whom.

Meals and food choices

While you are in hospital, breakfast, lunch and an evening meal will be served to you at your bedside. Most hospitals use a tick-box menu card, allowing you to express some level of choice in the food you are served and catering for most dietary requirements. Sometimes restrictions will be placed on your eating and drinking by your doctors or dieticians.

Hospital food has certainly improved, but we would not be telling the truth if we said that patients are bowled over by the choice, taste and presentation! You are very welcome to ask friends and family to bring in snacks and food for you – in fact we would encourage it in most instances. Obviously, if you have been advised to stick to a specific diet by a doctor or dietician, you should check with them first that what you are being brought is safe for you to eat.

Meal times are increasingly 'protected'. This means that healthcare professionals do not visit patients during meal times unless in an emergency, and visitors are not generally permitted. This is because patients may otherwise miss food and drink (vital for their recovery) due to interruptions for blood tests, investigations, visits from doctors or other therapists, or visits from family and friends. Meal times are now often much more strictly 'policed' so that you do not see anyone, or have anything done to you, during this time.

Most wards will have a hot drinks trolley which you can usually use, though arrangements will vary between wards. Tea and coffee rounds are often done throughout the day and drinks are also offered with each meal. If you are unable to get to the trolley, you will be able to ask for help from a member of staff. There should also be a jug of water and a glass available at your bedside; ask a member of staff if the water needs to be refilled.

Receiving visitors

Most wards in the hospital have set visiting hours. This is to make sure that patients have enough time to eat, rest and receive treatment, and to allow the doctors and nurses to complete their work. However, seeing friends or relatives in hospital is an important part of helping patients to stay cheerful and to obtain support and encouragement in adjusting to their new surroundings. We have included a separate chapter (Chapter 22) with information for people visiting patients in hospital.

CHAPTER NINE

The intensive care unit

The intensive care unit (ICU) is where the most unwell patients in the hospital are given medical and nursing care. Most hospitals have a specialist unit of this type, but it may be called the intensive treatment unit (ITU). Specialist ICUs in very big hospitals may have a prefix: a 'neuro-ICU' is, for example, for patients with neurological conditions, and a 'cardiac-ICU' is for people with heart conditions. A large number of patients require a stay in ICU – about a quarter of a million patients a year in England and Wales alone.

Admission to an ICU is often a daunting experience for patients and their loved ones. ICUs are truly active around the clock, with patients having constant monitoring, continuous medication and other medical procedures. The need for high levels of care means that the lights are on for most of the day and night. Monitors and machines frequently beep and chime, and by necessity the wards are often open plan to allow easy access to patients at all times. In this chapter we explain some of the reasons for admission to an ICU and the types of treatment and monitoring used. We show what you might expect if you or a member of your family require admission to such a unit.

Why are people admitted to the ICU?

Admissions to the intensive care unit, like other admissions to hospital, may be planned or unplanned. A planned admission may occur after an elective ('planned') procedure; for example, after major surgery (such as transplant surgery or the removal of a large cancer) the surgical and anaesthetic team may realise that the patient will require intensive monitoring and therapy to recover in those important first couple of days after the operation and 'book' an ICU bed. This is particularly important for patients who are already known to be frail, or who have other illnesses.

Unplanned admissions to ICU occur because of emergency illnesses or injuries. A patient may be taken to ICU immediately after admission via the emergency department (because of serious trauma, poisoning or overwhelming infection, for example) or following the worsening of a medical condition that has been identified in another hospital ward (such as kidney failure or respiratory failure). Very occasionally, patients with more unusual conditions may need to be moved from one hospital to another which has a specialised ICU (for example, a neuro-ICU), as described above.

The ICU team

The most obvious difference between an ICU and other wards is that most patients on the ICU have their own dedicated nurse monitoring and caring for them constantly. The number and make-up of the team of doctors is also slightly different to that found on general medical and surgical wards. The doctors are usually dual-qualified, most frequently in intensive care and anaesthesia. There is quite a lot of cross-over in the skill-sets required in these two areas. Many of the patients are anaesthetised on intensive care and therefore need expert input to manage their airways, breathing and circulation. The doctors may be specialists in other areas of medicine as well – particularly acute or respiratory medicine – for similar reasons.

Usually, the whole team carries out two ward rounds a day. In addition, the hospital infection team usually do their own ICU ward round every day, providing expert input on the prevention

and treatment of infections. These doctors are usually microbi-
ologists. Other specialist teams may come to see patients and
give opinions – including, perhaps, the surgical teams who did
the operation on the patient, or the cardiology team to give an
opinion on a patient's heart function. In addition to the nursing
and medical teams, many other healthcare professionals have an
input into the care of intensive care patients, including pharmacists, dieticians and physiotherapists. The ICU is therefore a very
busy environment. However, the clinical staff will do their utmost
to maintain a calm atmosphere.

Each patient may be seen by two or three teams of doctors
every day. No single team is 'in charge', but each has its own
specific responsibilities and works in collaboration with others.
For example, after a major operation to remove an abdominal
cancer, the surgeon will usually decide when to remove the drain
from the abdomen and when to start feeding the patient a normal diet. However, the ICU doctors will make decisions about
ventilator settings, pain control and fluid management.

When intensive care patients are awake, visiting healthcare
professionals should introduce themselves to the patient, and
if the patient is asleep or anaesthetised, they should introduce
themselves to any family members and friends who are present.
Understanding what each of these different teams are doing
can be confusing for both patients and relatives. As we describe
above, different decisions may be being made by different teams.
However teams will, whenever possible, be keen to explain what
aspects of care they are reviewing and what they are advising.

It is generally easier to direct questions initially to the ICU
team, as they are always present on the unit. The nurse caring
for the patient will usually be able to answer many questions,
and can also arrange a meeting with the ICU doctors as necessary. The condition of patients in intensive care can change very
quickly, so being regularly updated is important for patients and

relatives. The hard questions are often the most important, and while it may be difficult to listen to the answers, the process of understanding what is happening is important for everyone. Questions may need to be asked, and the answers heard, several times before they sink in. Everyone is naturally very anxious and this can make it harder to understand what is happening and also harder to remember the answers that have been given. Never be afraid to ask questions again, or to ask for answers to be repeated or given in a different way until you understand. Some key questions that may help are listed in Box 9.

> **Box 9** *Useful questions for patients and relatives to ask in intensive care*
>
> **General questions**
> - What is the diagnosis? Has this changed at all?
> - Is the patient getting better or worse?
> - Are the lungs/kidney/heart and circulation working or do they need support?
> - Is there any sign of the patient waking up yet? When are they likely to wake up?
> - What are the risks of the current treatment options?
> - How long will it be before signs of recovery might be seen?
>
> **Examples of very specific questions**
> - What does that device do?
> - What are these tubes for?
> - Is the patient in pain?
> - Do they know I am here? Can they hear me?

What happens in intensive care?

Patients in ICU are constantly checked by their own nurse and monitored closely by a number of medical devices (see Table 1).

Table 1 Medical devices frequently used in the ICU

Device	What it is and what it does
Cannula	A small plastic tube inserted using a needle into one of the more superficial veins on the hand, arm and occasionally leg. It is used to give drugs and fluids, and can stay in place for a number of days. Cannulas are sometimes referred to as drips, intravenous (IV) catheters or 'venflons' (a brand name).
Central venous line	A plastic tube inserted using a longer needle, usually into one of the larger neck veins, or less commonly into one of the veins near the groin. The tip of the tube opens into one of the very large veins in the body, near the heart. This is a very useful device, allowing the administration of certain drugs and second-by-second monitoring of the patient's blood pressure in their veins. Any patient receiving 'parenteral nutrition' (nutrition given intravenously) is also likely to need a central venous line to receive it. Regular blood samples can be taken from the line and it can usually stay in place for about seven to ten days.
Urinary catheter	A plastic tube inserted using lubricant gel through the urethra (where urine comes out of the body – the penis in men, just in front of the vagina in women) and into the bladder. It is used to drain urine when the patient cannot use their bladder, and allows monitoring of urine volume and thus kidney function. Most catheters can stay in place for a week or more before needing to be changed.
Arterial line	A plastic tube inserted using a needle, usually into the artery on the underside of the wrist. It is

Continued ...

Continued from previous page

	used to provide accurate blood pressure readings and to take blood samples for analysis of the levels of oxygen, carbon dioxide and acid in the blood. It can stay in place for up to a week.
Endotracheal tube	A plastic tube inserted through the mouth and into the windpipe while a patient is unconscious, and then connected to a ventilator (breathing machine). It is used to make sure the windpipe stays open, to deliver oxygen and other gaseous drugs into the lungs, and to protect the lungs from vomit or other secretions when a patient is unconscious. It can stay in place for as long as is needed, but may sometimes need to be changed. If a patient requires one for a very long time, it may be changed to a 'tracheostomy tube'. This is placed directly into the windpipe through the skin of the throat, rather than via the mouth, and is used only in those patients for whom a ventilator will be required for a long period.
Nasogastric tube	A plastic tube inserted using lubricant gel through the nostril, down the back of the throat and into the stomach. It is used to drain stomach contents when the bowel is not working properly or is blocked, and to provide liquid feed directly into the stomach when a patient cannot swallow safely.
Surgical drain	If the patient has fluid collecting in their chest or abdomen, a tube may be put in place to drain the fluid away. This often needs to be done after major surgery. The fluid is measured and samples are sent to the laboratory to help with making an accurate diagnosis.

Monitoring provides detailed information on, among other things: blood pressure, heart rate, breathing rate, temperature, the volume of urine that the body is making hour by hour, blood oxygen level and lung function. In addition, regular blood samples are taken for blood tests. Patients also receive powerful drugs to support them through critical periods of illness. For example, drugs can be used to improve a patient's blood pressure, reduce brain swelling or treat severe infections. Machines can be used to take over breathing, the role of the kidneys, or even some of the role of the heart in pumping blood around the body for a short period of time (see Table 2).

Infection is always a major concern for patients in the ICU, as people often lose many of their body's own defence mechanisms when they are critically ill. Patients are also particularly vulnerable to infection, because their skin is breached in multiple places by plastic devices (such as cannulas, used to give intravenous medication), providing easy routes into the blood stream for bacteria. A patient's cough reflex and the ability of the lungs to clear secretions may also be impaired by the presence of a breathing tube. Minimising the risk of infection in intensive care is therefore very important to the healthcare professionals who work there. In some ICUs you may see lines drawn on the floor around the beds; these mark areas where no one can enter without wearing a disposable gown and gloves. Visitors may also be asked to follow these rules.

Why are patients unconscious?

Many patients in intensive care are unconscious. This is some-times as a result of their underlying medical condition, but most patients are deliberately kept heavily sedated or even under a full general anaesthetic (as one would be during an opera-tion). This is done using strong pain killers (usually morphine or morphine-like drugs) for those who may be in pain, sedatives

Table 2 Patient support machines in intensive care

Machine	What it is and what it does
Ventilator	A fairly large machine that sits near the head of an unconscious patient and is attached via tubing into the mouth of the patient to support their breathing. Air, sometimes rich in oxygen, is pushed into the lungs, and then drawn out again with the waste carbon dioxide. Sometimes called a breathing machine or artificial lung, a ventilator can also deliver certain inhaled drugs.
Dialysis machine or haemofilter	A large machine that sits beside the bed and is attached to a type of central line. This machine replaces the function of the kidneys in patients whose kidneys are not working properly. It takes blood out of the body, then 'washes' it to remove the build-up of natural waste products, getting rid of these and returning the 'cleaned' blood back into the patient.
Pumps and pump stand	Small pumps can control the infusion of different drugs into the body through tubing that runs into cannulas or a central line. These drugs include sedatives, painkillers, antibiotics and drugs to help the heart and the circulation (known as inotropes and vasopressors). Clear fluid is also given to keep the patient hydrated (since they are unlikely to be able to drink fluids), and sometimes intravenous (parenteral) nutrition, which looks like a bag of a milky-looking solution. If blood transfusions are needed in intensive care, these will also be on the pump stand. A rack of pumps is usually placed near the head of the patient.

(such as drugs used for a general anaesthetic during operations), or a mixture of both. Being kept in this unconscious state allows patients to be supported in a much more intensive way, keeping them safe and free from pain. Their breathing can be taken over by a machine, which in turn reduces the burden that breathing has on the rest of the body. You may find this surprising, but breathing is actually 'work'! Being kept sedated means that the experience of intensive care is much less distressing than it would be if the patient was awake; many patients do not remember anything about their time in intensive care and the numerous procedures that may have occurred during their stay. However, there can be side-effects from very long periods of sedation, including confusion and, on occasion, psychological problems after waking (see below).

Making decisions on behalf of patients who are unconscious is obviously difficult. Some of the most difficult decisions in the ICU need to be made when patients are not getting better, despite everything possible being done; a decision about when to withdraw treatment may need to be made. Because of the complex nature of these decisions, guidelines govern how doctors should make decisions about the care of patients who are not able to make these decisions for themselves (see Box 10).

Visiting patients in the ICU

Visiting times in intensive care are usually a little more relaxed than in general wards, because patients are so unwell and their condition can change quickly. However, there is often a limit on the number of visitors who can be with a patient at any one time and visiting may be restricted to close relatives. This is partly because staff need more space around the patient's bedside than in other wards in the hospital and partly due to the need to minimise the risk of infection. The use of alcohol gel to sanitise the hands of healthcare professionals and visitors before they touch a patient is essential. Visitors and staff should also regularly wash their hands in the sink with soap and water, particularly if there is

---

Box 10 *Summary of General Medical Council guidelines for making decisions for unconscious patients*

- Doctors must make care of the patient their first concern, treat patients with respect and dignity, and not discriminate against them.
- They must consider which options for treatment (including the option of no treatment) would provide overall clinical benefit for the patient and would be least restrictive of the patient's future choices.
- They must take into account any previous advance statements made by the patient expressing their preferences.
- They must take into account the views of anyone the patient may have asked the doctor to discuss their care with, or who has legal authority to make a decision on the patient's behalf. In some cases, a representative might be appointed to represent the patient.
- They should take into account the views of people close to the patient, including close relatives, on what the patient's wishes might be.

---

any risk of bodily fluids (for example, saliva, blood or urine) having got onto the skin. It is absolutely critical that visitors follow any advice that staff give about hand washing, not touching, or wearing gloves, masks or gowns when seeing the patient. The procedures may seem excessive to you, and it may feel quite upsetting to have physical barriers between you and your loved one, but everything possible must be done to protect patients from infection.

Recovering after being in intensive care

The majority of patients in intensive care 'step-down' either to an ordinary hospital ward or to a high dependency unit once they have passed the most critical point in their illness. A high dependency unit or critical care unit is a 'half-way house' between ICU and a normal hospital ward, with a nurse for every two or three patients and more monitoring than on a normal ward. It is extremely rare for patients to return home directly from the ICU.

Depending on the length of stay in intensive care, there may be a need for rehabilitation once a patient leaves the unit. This is most commonly due to muscle weakness affecting the arms, legs or other parts of the body, including sometimes the breathing muscles or even the muscles involved with speech. Over half of patients who are admitted to the ICU for more than a week need rehabilitation to restore muscle strength. They will require help from different healthcare professionals after their discharge from intensive care; this may include physiotherapy for arm, leg or breathing weakness, and speech and language therapy for difficulties in speaking.

Another common effect of a prolonged intensive care stay is psychological disturbance, which can affect as many as one in four intensive care patients. This is frequently experienced as anxiety or low mood, but may also become apparent through difficulties with memory. Relatives should be aware that patients in an ICU may experience very intense dreams, sometimes nightmares, which can affect them during their stay and afterwards. Patients who are discharged from the ICU also need to be aware that psychological symptoms can manifest in various, sometimes subtle, ways. These include poor concentration, muddled thinking, irrational anger, irritability, tearfulness, nightmares, and sometimes feelings of numbness or purposeful avoidance of any activities that might spark a memory of the intensive care episode. These symptoms, which at the extreme end of the range might indicate possible post-traumatic stress disorder, can occur weeks or even months after people are discharged. Fortunately, there are well-established psychological and medical treatments for such symptoms.

It is useful for both patients and their relatives to understand that experiences of this kind are part of the illness and a result of the time in intensive care. It does not matter how tough a person is, or whether they have had psychological problems in the past; psychological symptoms can arise in anyone. No one should feel that they are being 'weak' if they have such feelings. Patients who do experience psychological symptoms or who feel that they need further support after their discharge from intensive care should seek help from their GP in the first instance if they have returned home, or from their hospital doctors if they are an inpatient on another ward.

Sources of further information and support

Many ICUs run follow-up clinics for discharged patients, in which medical and psychological symptoms can be reviewed. If there are symptoms such as weakness, difficulty in speaking or psycho-logical problems, these can be reviewed and further support and treatment can be arranged. Even if a patient is not offered an appointment in one of these clinics following discharge, contact-ing the ICU (by telephone or email) will be a very good first step in getting the help the person needs.

Relatives play a key role in the rehabilitation of patients – after discharge from hospital in general, and particularly after discharge from intensive care. Muscle weakness and psycho-logical side-effects often leave a patient needing a high level of support in the immediate period after discharge. Patients who have been very unwell and have spent time in intensive care will also recover more slowly than other patients, and will need much more practical day-to-day help in the weeks and months after returning home.

Beyond the hospital and a patient's own network of friends and relatives, there are several independent organisations that provide a useful forum for discussion and information. Two of the most active are 'ICUsteps' (Intensive Care Unit Support Teams for Ex-Patients) and the Intensive Care Society (ICS), which have useful resources designed for patients and relatives (see Appendix). These independent organisations provide support for patients themselves and for their loved ones. While the patients have gone through the illness, their relatives and friends will have spent an anxious time during their period in ICU and may also want some help. Providing support and help to patients following their discharge from intensive care can place significant demands on friends and family, so do seek support when needed.

Tests and
investigations

CHAPTER TEN

Understanding risk and making choices

The chapters in this section, and the next, describe some of the investigations and treatments that you might have in hospital: various kinds of medication, radiotherapy, operations, endoscopy, MRI scans and blood transfusions, to name just a few. When deciding whether or not to undergo a specific investigation or treatment, or when choosing from among several options, you and your medical team will need to consider the advantages and disadvantages of each one. This involves thinking about the likely benefits and also about any risks or side-effects that the treatments entail. This chapter aims to help you understand these issues, so that you can be actively involved in making decisions about your care. We recommend that you read this chapter before you read about any specific investigations or treatments that you may be asked to consider. We start by explaining what is meant by 'risk', and how it is expressed.

What do we mean by risk?

Risk can be defined as the likelihood of something happening which causes harm. We all take risks, every day, even if they are only small. Generally, this is because we consider that the potential benefits outweigh the possible dangers. We may travel every day by car, train or bus, even though we understand that with each journey there is a small chance we may be involved in an accident. The small risk is justified by the significant gain of being able to travel to work, visit our friends and go on holiday. Some people enjoy sports or other adventurous activities such as horse riding, knowing that there is an inherent risk but feeling that the enjoyment they get offsets that risk.

Our decisions about risk in everyday life are influenced by past experience, our estimates of how dangerous an activity is, and the amount of control or self-determination we have in managing that risk. For instance, many people feel safer in a car that they are driving themselves than in a plane flown by someone else and entirely outside their personal control. In fact, mile for mile flying is very much safer than driving. We also overestimate the risk of events that are prominently reported in the media – so we worry about the risk of terrorism or shark attacks, but not the risks of obesity or alcohol use, which cause many more deaths.

Risk in healthcare

In hospital, both the patient and their medical team have to be sure that the benefits of an investigation or treatment outweigh the risks. Sometimes this is very clear cut. For example, the benefits of an operation to remove a life-threatening cancer are likely to clearly outweigh the risks involved. But what about deciding to take a daily tablet to reduce the future risk of heart attack, an event you may never actually suffer in practice? The decision becomes more difficult, and it is even more important to understand the potential risks and benefits involved. This can be challenging, as specific information may not be available – especially about the risks and benefits to you personally – but over time doctors and researchers have gained a very good understanding of the benefits and risks of most common investigations and treatments. Ultimately, what you want to know is what will actually happen to you, which is impossible to predict with certainty. However, knowing what generally happens with a particular operation or test gives a good basis for making your own decision.

Most treatments available on the NHS have been given thousands or even millions of times before, so there is plenty of information available on how well they work and any adverse effects they might have. All medication comes with an information sheet from which you can learn what the medicine is intended to do, as well as the potential adverse effects such as feeling drowsy, dizzy, sick and so on. Most hospitals will have advice leaflets describing specific operations or investigations, which doctors may give out when first discussing operations or other procedures; patients can then go away and read about the suggested benefits and risks. Some of these leaflets can be alarming, because they try to list all possible problems without telling you how often these problems occur, or how serious the consequences might be, but they remain a good source of information and remind us that nearly all treatments have side-effects and risks.

Specialised charities and groups are another very important source of information, and there is of course a massive amount of information on the internet. While there are some excellent health-related websites, which present clear evidence-based information, there are also many unregulated sites, which may include inaccurate or confusing information. We provide links to some credible, established web resources in the Appendix to this book.

Regardless of the information sources used, working out what it all means for you as an individual is probably best done by talking the decision over with a sympathetic and knowledgeable GP, a hospital doctor, a nurse or another healthcare professional. Many units have specialised nurses who know a great deal about their specialist area and who have seen many other patients with the same condition. They are usually an excellent source of information, and are often experienced at discussing risk and benefit in very human terms. GPs are also excellent at seeing 'the whole person' and putting any treatment or investigation into a personal context for you. Never be worried about asking the doctors or nurses looking after you what information they have or would recommend, and where you can access it – and for their thoughts and opinions.

Giving informed consent

When you or a loved one are considering having a procedure or test, or starting a new treatment, you need to know and understand the benefits and risks to help you make an informed decision about whether or not to proceed. If you then agree to the procedure, you are giving 'informed consent'.

Consent to treatment is the principle that you must give your permission before you receive any type of medical treatment, whether it is a simple blood test, a drug or a major operation. To do so, you must first consider the risks and benefits. The principle of consent is an important part of medical ethics and human rights. You give your consent to the person directly responsible for your treatment. This might be a phlebotomist taking a blood sample, your GP prescribing new medication, or the anaesthetist who is about to place an epidural injection into your spine to reduce pain during childbirth.

In many cases, consent is very straightforward and is little more than agreeing to the procedure or treatment. If you roll up your sleeve and offer your arm to the nurse taking blood, they can reasonably assume that you are giving consent. If your GP explains that a drug will help your asthma and you say 'yes, I think I should try that', they will assume that you have given consent. Consent can be implied by a nod, or by raising your arm towards the needle, or by verbal agreement. However, if you are going to have a more significant intervention such as an endoscopy (see Chapter 13) or an operation (see Chapter 15), the consent will be more formal. You will be asked to sign a consent form which states that you have had everything explained to you and that you understand the risks. Unless it is an emergency, the consent procedure should be started well in advance, so that you have time to study any information about the procedure and ask questions. In fact you might consent on one day and then be asked on the day of your procedure to 'confirm your consent' by re-signing the form.

Thinking about what matters to you

Clinical studies, audits and large databases provide us with detailed information about the risks and benefits of specific treatments, and understanding this information gives you and your medical team the foundations for making a decision. However, data drawn from any of these sources usually relates to large and sometimes quite specific populations. An example is the excellent study that helped introduce a type of screening test for bowel cancer. This study included over 170,000 people (a population the size of Ipswich), aged between 55 and 64 years. It showed that the test helped reduce that population's risk of bowel cancer and was safe. But just because the test helped that population as a whole, will it help you? What happens if you find it difficult to lie flat (which the test requires) because of breathing problems? Does it matter if you are 75, and therefore older than the population tested? Whenever considering a test or treatment, you and your clinicians should consider your particular circumstances and decide how the evidence relates specifically to you.

Imagine two patients with arthritis in their left knee, both considering a total knee replacement. The first patient is 80 and has really bad arthritis. It hurts every time she walks more than 50 metres. However, she is also limited by her heart failure and rarely walks outside the home. The pain goes away with painkillers. The anaesthetic doctors tell her that having an anaesthetic is very high risk because of her heart. The second patient is in his early fifties and plays two games of tennis and two rounds of golf each week. He has mild arthritis, but increasingly cannot finish his tennis match, is playing less golf, and is putting on weight due to taking less exercise. He is otherwise healthy and the anaesthetic doctors see no problems at all for him having the anaesthetic.

The X-ray of the knee of the first patient shows that she 'needs' the knee replacement a lot more than the second patient does; her knee is almost useless. However, the operation carries some risks and her knee problems are not greatly affecting her daily life. She decides not to have an operation because it is not worth taking the high risk for a small benefit. The X-ray of the knee of the second patient shows much less damage, and his knee problems overall are much less serious. However, the damaged knee has a big impact on his daily life. He therefore decides to have the operation. He is relatively lower risk, but has a potentially high benefit. In both cases, the patients have to decide what is most important to them and their doctors need to think about the whole patient and not just their knees.

Ways of expressing risks and benefits

Any discussion or consideration of risk with a doctor or health-care professional is likely to involve a lot of numbers. Every day, the tabloid media report 'scientific findings' and give them the most alarmist of interpretations; a certain food may be labelled as 'doubling' your risk of cancer, or a new wonder drug reduces your stroke risk 'by half'. The manner in which we talk about risks and benefits and the way we use numbers greatly affect how we make decisions.

Let's consider an example. Suppose there was a drug that cut your risk of having a heart attack by half. That certainly sounds good and you might be quite keen to take it. Halving your risk of a heart attack sounds like a lot! But suppose you were then told about a drug which reduced your risk of a heart attack from 2 in

1,000 to 1 in 1,000. You might be less keen? Finally, suppose you were told that you and 999 other people just like you all have to take a drug every day for a year to prevent just one of you 1,000 people from having a heart attack? And that we do not know whether or not you are one of the 998 who is never going to have a heart attack anyway, or the person who is going to have a heart attack despite taking the medicine, or the one person who is saved by the drug!

All these statements can mean more or less the same thing, which sounds extremely confusing. The confusion comes from the different ways of talking about risk:

Reducing your risk by half. This expresses 'relative risk' or 'relative risk reduction'. This is a common way of stating the effect of a drug or intervention because it sounds the most impressive. It is true – the drug does halve your chance of having a heart attack.

Reducing your risk from 2 in 1,000 to 1 in 1,000. This is the 'absolute benefit' or the 'absolute risk reduction'. This is more useful information for you, as it shows that your risk is reduced from 'very small' to 'very, very small'.

Treating 1,000 people to save one heart attack. The final statement, which is increasingly used by scientists and doctors, is called the 'numbers needed to treat' (NNT). This can be very helpful, because it states things far more from the patient's viewpoint. So in this scenario we would say, 'If there were 1,000 people just like you, and you all took the medicine every day for a year, we would stop one of you from having a heart attack.' A similar concept is the 'number needed to harm'. It allows a surgeon, for example, to say to someone, 'If I did this operation on 50 people like you, one of them would suffer a serious complication but the other 49 would go home the next day with no problems.'

Words, numbers, percentages and proportions

Numbers associated with explaining risk can be presented in other ways. Your doctor may talk about percentages (the number of times things happen out of 100 – for instance, 10%); proportions expressed as a decimal (0.1); frequencies expressed in numbers (one in ten) or in words ('quite common'). Using words to describe risk is helpful for some people, but phrases such as 'common' or 'very rare' can be interpreted in different ways, so we personally recommend using numbers as well as words to make things clearer. If you do not understand, or if you think the person providing you with information is not being clear, then you should ask them to clarify or try a different approach. Using numbers is often the easiest, alongside expressing what would happen to a group of people who are all having the treatment you are discussing. Rather than worry about percentages you can ask, 'So, how many people out of 100 does this happen to?' or 'How many people need to take this tablet for one of them to get the benefit?' Thinking about the numbers of people you know, or who live near you, can be a good way of getting a sense of what these numbers mean in practice (see Table 3).

Table 3 Assessing risks and benefits

Natural frequency	Description
From 1 in 1 to 1 in 10	Someone in your family
From 1 in 10 to 1 in 100	Someone in your street
From 1 in 100 to 1 in 1,000	Someone in a village
From 1 in 1,000 to 1 in 10,000	Someone in a small town
Less than 1 in 100,000	Someone in a large town

Your doctor may use 'decision aids' to help explain risk. These can be effective because they tend to use pictures or diagrams (see Figure 2), which you may find easier to understand than words and numbers. You may also be given leaflets and other written sources of information to support the conversations you have. Some questions you may like to ask are presented in Box 11.

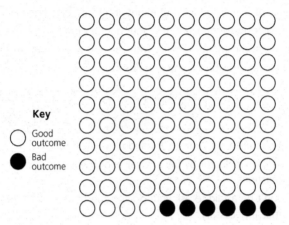

Key

○ Good outcome

● Bad outcome

Figure 2 Example of a decision aid: 'Here are 100 people who have the suggested operation.'

Box 11 *Questions you should ask about your treatment*

- What are my treatment options?
- What would happen if I didn't have any treatment?
- Which treatment is most common for my disease or my condition?
- What side-effects can I expect?
- What risks and benefits are associated with the treatment?
- What would happen if I delayed my treatment?
- How long will the treatment take?
- What is the cost of the treatment? (if applicable)
- Is there anything I should avoid during treatment?
- How will I know if the treatment has worked/is working?
- Will my job or lifestyle be affected?

Finally, remember that all treatments and investigations have both risks and benefits. Often the risks are very small indeed, but for more serious treatments you need to think about both. For instance, a drug might show benefits in terms of reducing the chance of a heart attack, but might also cause bleeding in some of the people who take it. It is your doctor's job to explain both benefits and risks and to work with you and your family to come to the best decision for you (see Box 12).

Box 12 *Discussing decisions with your doctor or other healthcare professional*

- Be honest with your doctor about how you feel.
- Help your doctor by being clear about your concerns and questions.
- Don't be afraid to ask your doctor questions – more than once if necessary.
- Write things down, or ask your doctor to, so that you have something to refer to afterwards.
- Ask your doctor to explain things in various ways. They may have a diagram or be able to use different words that make more sense to you.
- Take somebody with you to your appointments. They may remember things afterwards that you have forgotten, and may also have ideas about questions to ask.
- Take your time, during the appointment and after it, when weighing up the pros and cons and considering what to do.
- Ask for reliable sources, where you can look for more information.
- If questions occur to you after your appointment, write them down so you can ask them next time.
- Consider requesting another appointment if you would like time to go away and 'mull things over' before deciding on a course of action.

Can I ask my doctor to make a decision for me?

Ultimately, the decision to have a screening test or an investigation, to start a medicine or to have an operation rests with just you, the patient. It is really helpful to be given information, and to understand it. The days of medical paternalism, in which the doctor makes all the decisions without involving the patient at all, are largely in the past.

However, we urge a note of caution. As keen as we are to empower and inform patients, families and carers, and to engage them in decision-making, we are also aware that it can be overwhelming when you are ill; you may prefer to rely on the advice of your doctor or other member of staff. You may just feel that you cannot make a sensible decision because you feel too ill or because it is too complicated. In that case, it is absolutely fine to ask your doctor what they would recommend and to allow them to shoulder some of that responsibility. You should trust the doctors, nurses and other healthcare professionals treating you; the vast majority go to work wanting nothing more than to care for their patients and get the very best for them. If your doctor or nurse is strongly recommending something, then it is probably the best course of action.

CHAPTER ELEVEN

History and examination

Once you have arrived in hospital, one of the first tasks for your team of doctors is to find out what is wrong with you. They may already have letters from your GP, or the findings of initial assessments in the emergency department, but they will generally want to make their own assessment of your problems. Only then can they confirm a diagnosis and decide what treatment you may need. The most critical part of this assessment process is asking questions about you and your illness and examining you.

An experienced doctor will often be able to make a diagnosis simply by talking to you and examining you. However, they will also probably carry out further investigations such as blood tests and scans to confirm the diagnosis or to guide treatment. We are now able to benefit from amazing technological developments such as ultrasound scanning, CT scans and MRI (magnetic resonance imaging) (all explained in Chapter 13), and a host of rapid blood tests. When required, even more advanced tests such as nuclear imaging or genetic analysis can be performed, some of which are described in more detail in the next two chapters. However, taking a history and performing an examination remain the mainstay of diagnosis.

Healthcare professionals often refer to 'taking a history'. The 'history' is the story of your illness, including your immediate problem as well as any previous medical problems, your family history and your social circumstances. Giving a history and being examined is often the first experience a patient has when coming into hospital and it can be unsettling for some. A stranger – albeit a doctor or other healthcare professional – will ask a series of questions, some of them straightforward and obvious, others seemingly strange or embarrassingly intimate. It may not be immediately obvious why they wish to know about your personal habits. The examination almost always involves an inspection of the main body 'systems' – heart, lungs and digestive system – but will also focus on other areas relevant to your particular symptoms, such as the bones and joints or the nervous system. Being examined may require you to partially undress while the doctor inspects, listens to and feels various parts of your body.

Doctors are taught to set patients at their ease as much as possible, but it is perfectly natural that many people find an examination a strange and uncomfortable experience. Very few of us normally allow a stranger to be so intimate with us so rapidly. In this chapter we hope to make this process seem more familiar by explaining what is likely to happen.

Giving and taking a history

Taking a history is an art in itself, finely honed over many years of experience. You may notice this yourself – if a medical student or newly qualified doctor comes to talk to you, they may take 20 minutes to find out the information they need, whereas a more senior clinician may take only two or three minutes to obtain the same information. This ability to obtain the essential details while moving swiftly past information which is not relevant is a very difficult thing to teach and tends to require years of practice and thousands of patient encounters.

The medical history helps the clinician put your symptoms into context; a set of particular symptoms in a 22-year-old woman may well point to a different diagnosis to the same set of symptoms in an 82-year-old man. Your role as the patient, or as a supporting family member, is to 'give the history', which simply means telling the story as clearly as you can in your own words. If your medical history is complicated, it is helpful to keep a record of the main points and bring a copy with you to hospital.

A medical history can be divided into several sections. Not all doctors will take a history in the order listed below, but they will normally cover most, if not all, of these areas:

The presenting complaint

The doctor will generally begin with an open question – such as, 'Tell me why you've come to the hospital today' – to get your history in your own words. The answer you give to this question is known as the 'presenting complaint', which might be 'I have a pain in my chest' or 'I feel dizzy all the time'. The doctor will then try to find out all the symptoms that have been affecting you, and will probably ask more specific questions – 'How long has the pain been there?' or 'Is your dizziness made worse by stand-ing or lying?' – to confirm or rule out a diagnosis. The doctor will try to find out how long the problem has affected you, anything that makes it worse, anything that makes it better, and whether or not you have suffered anything similar before.

Your past medical history

The doctor will ask about any medical conditions that you have now or have had in the past, any previous hospital admissions, and any operations that you have undergone. The doctor will also be likely to ask specifically about some common conditions; it is surprising how many people forget to mention their high blood pressure or diabetes because they are so used to having the condition!

Drug history

The doctor will ask you about any prescription drugs or over-the-counter medication you are taking and if you have any allergies or sensitivities to medicines. This part of the history is vital, so it is very helpful if you can carry a piece of paper or a copy of your prescription with these details on it. This helps the doctors, nurses and pharmacists ensure that you receive your medication at the right dose while in hospital, and also gives them vital clues regarding your medical conditions and their severity. For example, two different patients may both have 'high blood pressure', but one may take a low dose of a single drug to control it and the other may be on three or four strong drugs. This information is very helpful in assessing the risks to the patient from their condition. We consider the medication history in more detail in Chapter 14.

Social history

Your doctor will want to understand a little about how you lead your life on a day-to-day basis. This gives them information about what may have caused your problem, and also helps them assess the potential impact of your condition on your life. They may ask whether you work, who you live with, what sort of housing you live in, and whether you need help with your daily activities. They will ask whether you smoke, drink alcohol or take recreational drugs. In some cases, they may also ask about your reproductive or sexual history. While you may feel awkward about answering some of these questions, it is important to be honest. Healthcare professionals are not there to judge you; they only ask these questions in order to get a better understanding of your illness.

Family history

Certain conditions 'run in the family', so the doctor may ask about these. Examples include heart disease, diabetes and some types of cancer.

Telling your story again and again

We know from talking to patients that it can be quite frustrating to be asked many of these questions several times by different people. For example, if you are admitted via the emergency department, you will probably see the triage nurse (see Chapter 6), then the emergency doctor, then a specialty doctor and several different members of the team. You may find that you have told the same story five or six times. This can be quite frustrating, especially when you are not well, and you may feel that you have been bombarded with the same questions over and over again. However, this happens because everyone involved in your care wants to be certain that they understand your story and have heard it in your own words. Different healthcare professionals may also ask questions that are new or asked slightly differently, which can bring more information and help them to work out what is wrong.

The medical examination

After taking your history, the doctor will usually perform an examination. As with history taking, there are various formats and each doctor has their particular routine. But when you are admitted to hospital, particularly if you come in through the emergency department, there are some parts of the body that your doctor will nearly always examine:

Hands, arms, face and neck

A doctor can tell a surprising amount from your hands. Fingernails can show signs of iron deficiency. The shape of the fingers, particularly if the finger tips are swollen like drumsticks, can suggest inflammatory conditions or certain cancers of the heart, lung or gastrointestinal systems. The palms can reveal anaemia or liver disease.

Your doctor will probably take your pulse at the wrist, the elbow or possibly at the neck. Pulses can be fast or slow, regular or irregular, weak or strong, and have various other characteristics, all of which provide information about how your heart is beating. Your doctor will check your blood pressure, and may examine your eyes and eyelids and look inside your mouth. They may look at the right side of your neck to check the pressure waves in your veins, and feel for your windpipe to make sure it is not displaced.

Heart and lungs

Your doctor will normally examine your heart and lungs. They will feel your chest for any abnormal movements and may use a finger to tap on your chest in various places. Many patients find that the tapping feels a little odd, but it enables the doctor to check for resonance or dullness under the chest wall. The lungs, for instance, should be full of air. If they sound dull rather than resonant, the lungs may have fluid in them as well as air, or one of the lungs may have collapsed.

Your doctor will then listen to your chest at various points, front and back, using a stethoscope. They will listen to the sounds made by your heart as it beats – whether they are loud or soft, and whether there are any extra sounds. The doctor will also listen to the character of your breathing, checking for additional sounds such as crackles or wheeze, which can suggest various lung problems.

Abdomen and groin

Your doctor may ask you to lie flat on the bed. They will then examine your abdomen to look for any signs of previous surgery, areas of pain, or unusual lumps or swellings. This can be slightly uncomfortable if they press deeply and it is important to say if it is painful. Do not 'be brave'– they need to know if you have pain, and where it is. Your doctor will specifically feel for the liver on the right of your abdomen, and for your spleen on the left. They may tap the abdomen (in a similar fashion to the chest) and listen with a stethoscope for the sounds your bowels are making. They may need to examine the groin for swellings or lumps, and in certain circumstances examine your genitalia and bottom.

Nervous system

Most patients who come into hospital via the emergency department will have their nervous system examined, if only briefly. A thorough examination of how the nerves inside your head and spine are working can take quite a long time. Unless your doctor is specifically concerned about a neurological condition, they will therefore probably perform a quick version involving what may seem some rather unusual requests. They may examine your pupils with a torch and check the movement of your eyes, check the sensation in your face, and ask you to close your eyes tightly and blow out your cheeks so that they can check your facial muscles. You may be asked to say some tongue-twisting phrases, and then to stick out your tongue and move it from side to side. They may quickly check your hearing. Finally, your doctor may check the power of your neck muscles and shoulders and the power, reflexes and sensation of your arms and legs.

Observations

The full history and examination takes place at the beginning of your hospital stay. However, staff will continue to check how you are feeling and whether you are in pain, to monitor your condition throughout your hospital stay. Observations of your 'vital signs' are a particularly important part of this. Observations are a batch of routine tests carried out as soon as you come into hospital and are likely to be repeated at regular intervals throughout the day for as long as you are in hospital. They consist of measuring your pulse (which indicates how fast your heart is beating), your blood pressure, your temperature, how many breaths you take in a minute, and sometimes your oxygen saturation. Pulse and oxygen saturation (which tells the medical staff how much oxygen is getting into your blood from your lungs) can both be measured by a small probe clipped onto one of your fingers, toes or even ear lobes. Your blood pressure is measured using a cuff around your arm. The nurse or healthcare assistant taking your observations will count how quickly or slowly you are breathing. These tests are all quick and painless. They may become repetitive, but these basic measurements of your body's functions can give the clinical team looking after you vital information on your general well-being. If all these tests are normal, you may well still be 'ill', but it is very unlikely that you are in any real danger.

CHAPTER TWELVE

Blood tests and samples

You can learn a lot from testing bodily fluids! This is why most patients admitted to hospital, or even visiting for an outpatient appointment, will be asked to provide samples of their urine and blood, and sometimes their stools (poo) or other bodily fluids such as sputum (mucus from the throat or lungs). Providing these samples is important in helping your clinicians find out what is wrong and how best to treat the problem. For some people, particularly those who are very unwell, blood tests become part of the daily hospital routine, but their importance is not always explained. This chapter describes how and why various laboratory tests are performed, starting with blood and then moving on to urine and stool tests.

Blood tests

Blood tests involve inserting a small needle into a vein and using a syringe or vacuum container to withdraw a small sample of blood. The blood sample is usually divided into a variety of different-coloured bottles, each containing different chemical agents. This allows several tests to be performed with one blood sample.

The blood is sent to the hospital laboratories, where it is examined using microscopes and other equipment to measure the levels of various substances in it. As well as several different types of cells, your blood contains various proteins, hormones and salts. Illness can change the balance and amounts of these substances in different ways; the blood tests can help doctors to make a diagnosis or monitor changes in your disease. Blood tests are therefore a quick and relatively easy way to obtain a lot of information about how well your body is working. There are a multitude of blood tests available. Table 4 summarises some of the most common, and explains what each test can tell your doctor. Box 13 suggests some questions that you may like to ask about blood and other tests.

Table 4 Common blood tests and why they are performed

Test	What does it tell us?
Full blood count	The number of red cells, white cells and platelets are counted, the amount of haemoglobin assessed, and the size and volume of the red cells calculated. This provides information about conditions such as anaemia, infection or problems with the bone marrow.
Urea and electrolytes (U and Es)	This test assesses the amount of salts ('electrolytes') in the plasma, which can be altered in many conditions. The amount of two substances, called urea and creatinine, can also indicate how well the kidneys are functioning.
Liver function tests	If the liver is damaged or functioning incorrectly, it can release certain chemicals and enzymes into the blood. Some diseases and conditions can be diagnosed based on which of these chemicals have raised levels.
Blood clotting	The liver makes many proteins that help the blood to clot. If the level of these proteins in the blood is too low, or if the proteins are not formed correctly, there is a risk of bleeding. This test is frequently

Continued ...

Continued from previous page

	carried out in people taking 'blood thinning' medication such as warfarin or heparin, and in patients about to undergo surgery, when it is essential to know how well their blood is clotting.
Inflammation tests: C-reactive protein (CRP) and erythrocyte sedimentation rate (ESR)	Extra proteins are released when there is inflammation in the body, and these can be detected in the blood. For example, a protein called C-reactive protein is released when your body is under a lot of stress, such as when it is affected by infection or trauma.
Immunology	Some viruses, and antibodies to these viruses, can be detected in the blood, indicating specific types of infection such as hepatitis. Sometimes your body can also make antibodies to itself ('auto-immune conditions'). Measuring the levels of these antibodies can help diagnose auto-immune conditions such as rheumatoid arthritis.
Blood grouping	Blood cells have proteins on their surfaces called antigens. There are three common red cell antigens: A, B and Rhesus. Somebody with A and Rhesus is 'A Rhesus positive'; someone without A or B or Rhesus is 'O negative'. These are the basis of the different blood groups. If you might need a blood transfusion, your blood group needs to be established so that the correct blood can be given. (See Chapter 16 for more details.)

Box 13 *Questions to ask about your tests*

- What is the test for?
- What will it tell you about my illness?
- How long will it take before the test results are available?
- How do I find out the results? Who will tell me the results?

Some blood tests can be affected by what you have eaten, so you may be asked not to eat or drink anything other than water before a blood test. Occasionally, you may also be asked to stop taking certain medicines. For children, a local anaesthetic cream may be put on the area beforehand. In general, though, no specific preparation is needed.

How is blood taken?

Blood samples are usually taken by a specifically trained healthcare professional called a phlebotomist, but they may also be done by a doctor, nurse or other trained member of staff. The person carrying out the blood test should have washed their hands beforehand and be wearing gloves. A suitable vein is found – usually on the inside of the arm or on the back of the hand. To make the vein full of blood, a tight band called a tourniquet is placed just above the vein. The skin is then cleaned, and a needle is inserted through the skin and into the vein. The needle is then connected either to a syringe or to a small blood bottle, and blood is taken. The tourniquet is removed, and the needle is taken out. Cotton wool is placed over the area, and pressure is applied for a minute or so to prevent bruising; you may be asked to press gently on top of the cotton wool with your spare hand. A plaster or other dressing may be put onto the small wound to keep it clean.

When the needle is inserted, you may feel a sharp scratch or you may feel very little. If you have had lots of blood tests before from the same vein, the scarring on the vein can make the process a bit more uncomfortable. Either way, once the needle has been inserted, it may be slightly uncomfortable but it will not be painful. Most people find it easier to look away when the needle is being put in. The healthcare professional taking the blood will probably also talk to distract you.

Age and certain medical conditions such as kidney disease can make it harder to get blood from the vein. There are therefore several different-sized needles and methods available for taking blood. There are also times when it is necessary to know how much oxygen is in the blood. To measure this, blood needs to be taken from an artery rather than a vein. The artery used is typically on the wrist, and a doctor will usually perform this test as it is slightly more difficult and slightly more risky, compared to standard blood tests.

For some tests, such as to measure the amount of sugar in your blood, a 'finger prick test' may be required instead of taking blood from a vein. In this case, a very small needle is used on the end of your finger, and the resulting drop of blood is squeezed onto a special strip of paper and read by a machine.

What are the risks of blood tests?

Whenever a needle is inserted into the skin, there is a slight risk of infection entering the body. This risk is minimised if the area is properly cleaned beforehand and the person taking the blood washes their hands and wears gloves. If these procedures have not been followed, do remind the person concerned, or ask if there is a reason why they are not doing so (which is unlikely but possible).

When the needle is removed, there is likely to be very slight bleeding and this can form a bruise. This is minimised if you press firmly over the site with cotton wool for about a minute afterwards.

Many of us feel nervous about needles and seeing blood. However, some people are very afraid of needles and can become very anxious even at the thought of one. This is known as needle phobia. If you have a phobia of needles and think you may feel faint when having your blood taken, it is important that you let the healthcare professional know; they may suggest that you lie down while the blood sample is taken.

Urine samples

A urine test examines the chemical substances found in urine. A 'mid-stream' urine sample is usually required, which is done by placing a sterile pot into the stream of urine just after you have started to urinate. It can be a bit awkward to do this, especially for women. If you know you are going to need to produce a urine sample, you may also wish to try and avoid emptying your bladder shortly beforehand.

The urine sample is then analysed by the nurse or doctor, who places a 'urine dipstick' into the pot. The dipstick has several different-coloured sections that have been primed with different chemicals; these change colour depending on what has been detected in the urine. Specifically, urine tests can be used to look at the following:

- *Leucocytes and nitrites*. These suggest a urine infection.
- *Glucose*. This may be detected in people with diabetes.
- *Ketones*. These are seen in uncontrolled diabetes, or if someone is very dehydrated or in a starvation state.
- *Blood*. This may reflect contamination with menstrual blood in women, or can indicate a problem with the kidneys, such as trauma or a kidney stone. If blood is detected, the sample will usually be sent off for more detailed analysis under a microscope. About one in ten of the healthy population will have tiny amounts of blood in their urine; most of these people have nothing wrong with them.

- *Protein*. This may indicate kidney disease. If protein is identified, the sample will be sent off for further analysis alongside blood tests.

Urine tests are probably the most common tests performed in hospital. They will be performed on nearly all patients with diabetes or known chronic renal failure who are admitted to hospital, and on anyone who has experienced symptoms of a urinary tract infection, such as burning while urinating or needing to urinate more often than usual. All patients with abdominal pain will be asked to give a urine sample; so will most patients suffering a trauma, or complaining of blood in their urine. All women with possible gynaecological problems will undergo urine testing, as will all patients who have a fever or infection of unknown cause. Women of childbearing age will also have a pregnancy test done using a urine sample. To summarise, almost everyone who comes to hospital as a patient will be asked to provide a urine sample at some point during their visit!

Whenever one of the dipstick analysis tests shows a positive result, meaning that it could indicate signs of a disease, the urine sample will be sent to the laboratory for further analysis. If the urine is found to grow bacteria, the laboratory scientists will also find out which antibiotics the bacteria are most sensitive to, to ensure that the best antibiotic is given. Urine tests are very safe, with no associated risk other than potential difficulty in collecting the sample.

Stool samples

A stool (poo) sample is often required when people have problems with their bowels. These may include severe or long-term diarrhoea, blood in their stools, a change in their bowel habit or an illness after travelling abroad. When a stool sample is sent to the laboratory, it can be analysed for bacteria and parasites (sometimes seen as eggs or worms under a microscope). If bacteria are found, the sample is tested to assess which antibiotics the bacteria are sensitive to so that the right antibiotics can be prescribed. Stool can also be assessed for the presence of blood (faecal occult blood or FOB).

A stool sample is obtained by placing a small amount of stool into a container, using a little spoon attached to the lid of the container. The sample is then sent to the laboratory for further analysis, which may take several days. It can be a bit awkward to obtain the sample but this is another very safe test with no risks to you.

Other bodily fluids

Almost every fluid made by the body can be tested – the list is too long to go through every possible one. If fluid has accumulated in a joint, in the abdomen, around the lungs or around the heart, it may be aspirated (sucked out using a needle) and sent to the laboratory. If you are coughing up sputum or 'phlegm', it may be collected and sent. Any infected pus that leaks will be swabbed and sent to the microbiology team for 'culture' (growing any bacteria) and 'sensitivity' (seeing which antibiotics kill the bacteria). Wonderful amounts of information can be obtained in this way.

CHAPTER THIRTEEN

Looking inside
the body

Doctors can often work out what is wrong with you by asking questions, examining your body and using simple investigations such as blood tests. However, sometimes other tests are needed which look inside your body to find out more about your condition. Modern technology has significantly improved our capacity to examine the inside of the body in ever-greater detail while minimising the risks involved. The investigations described in this chapter form a valuable part of a doctor's toolkit to help decide what is wrong with you and plan your treatment. The two main ways of looking inside the body are:

- *Radiology*. Using X-rays and other types of scan to examine the body from the outside.
- *Endoscopy*. Looking inside the body using a long tube attached to a camera.

There are other ways of looking inside the body, some of which involve having an operation under general anaesthetic, but radiology and endoscopy are the most common. We focus here on their use to help make a diagnosis, although both are also sometimes used to provide treatment for specific conditions.

Radiology

The radiology department is where you go to have X-rays and other scans. Radiology machines come in various shapes and sizes, but all of them are designed to work from outside the body in order to look inside. Many of the investigations are very straightforward and take only a few minutes.

Many X-rays and other scans simply require you to take up a particular position and remain still while the scanner takes pictures. However, some radiology investigations require you to be given a type of dye or 'contrast medium' to get a more detailed picture of what is going on inside your body. These dyes are often given as an injection through a drip that a member of staff will place in your vein before the scan. Sometimes you may need to drink the contrast as a liquid, or it may be given to you some other way, such as via the rectum (your bottom), or through tubes or drains already placed in your body. As you can imagine, some of these procedures may feel a little embarrassing and uncomfortable, but any discomfort should be minor and brief.

There are two main groups of hospital staff involved in performing and analysing the results of radiology tests:

A radiographer is a healthcare professional who has received specialised professional training to perform scans. In the case of ultrasound, radiographers may also be trained to interpret the result of the scan and write a report of their findings. Other types of scan are generally sent to a radiologist to analyse.

A radiologist is a doctor who specialises in reviewing the pictures provided by a scan. Radiologists interpret the results of your scan and discuss the findings with the team of doctors looking after you. This conversation and their report on the test often help your doctors to decide what is wrong with you. Radiologists may also perform certain tests and treatments themselves.

Types of radiological test

The term 'radiological test' covers a number of types of investigation, using different machines and procedures:

Plain X-rays

X-rays are the most common radiology test. For instance, you may have a chest X-ray if you have a cough or are short of breath, or an X-ray of an arm or leg to see if it is broken. Having an X-ray is a bit like having a photo taken. Sometimes jewellery or clothing may need to be taken off. You will sit or lie down alongside the machine; then a small dose of X-ray radiation is sent through the area being examined towards the X-ray film on the other side of your body. This radiation travels more easily through soft tissue and air than it does through dense tissues like bone. This means that the amount of radiation that reaches the film on the other side of the body will depend on what type of body tissue it has passed through. This creates a picture of the various structures on the X-ray film. You may have seen X-rays of broken bones where the break is clearly visible. Previously X-rays were done using a type of film which was then 'developed', but modern technology means it can all be processed electronically and viewed on a computer. Often the radiographer will take more than one X-ray to get a different view of the same part of your body, but generally the whole process will be completed within a few minutes.

Ultrasound scans

Ultrasound scans work using the same principle as sonar on submarines. An ultrasound probe emits a very high frequency of sound waves, much higher than can be heard by human ears (hence the name '*ultra*sound'). These sound waves travel through parts of the body and are reflected by different bits of your body in different ways. The probe picks up the reflected sound waves, and a computer assembles them into an image, giving important information about the various organs within the body.

Ultrasound can be used in lots of different contexts. Some examples are pre-natal scanning of pregnant women to check the baby inside, scanning the abdomen to investigate the cause of abdominal pain, and scanning veins and arteries to ensure there are no clots, narrowings or swellings. The ultrasound machine can also help determine flow through these blood vessels. Nearly all scans are performed with you lying on a couch. The part of the body being examined will need to be exposed, then a type of jelly will be applied to the end of the ultrasound probe before the scan starts. (This can sometimes mean the tip of the probe is quite cold when it first touches your skin.) The person performing the scan will place the probe of the machine against your skin and move it around to look at different parts of the body underneath. Occasionally they may push a bit to try to see something more clearly, or ask you to hold your breath. Let them know if you find anything uncomfortable. The full scan can vary considerably in duration, from a few minutes to an hour or so, depending on what is being looked at and whether any interventions are planned. Depending on the part of the body being scanned, you may be asked not to eat beforehand, or you may be asked to drink plenty to make sure your bladder is full, which can have the effect of making the ultrasound picture of the pelvis clearer.

Computerised tomography (CT or CAT) scans

CT scanners make use of the same basic properties of radiation as X-rays. However, a CT scan involves a very large number of smaller X-ray images, taken from many different angles, which are then combined on a computer to create a large number of pictures of different areas of your body. Sometimes these are also referred to as CAT scans; CAT stands for 'computerised axial tomography'. This kind of scan uses a computer to create images of the inside of your body in more detail than is possible with a straightforward X-ray. For example, CT scans are used to image the brain after a stroke, or to search for the potential spread of certain cancers to other parts of the body.

A CT scan involves lying down on a relatively narrow, firm couch that is then moved in and out of a round window within a larger machine. You are moved slowly through something that looks rather like a large doughnut. You are not in a tunnel, so most patients do not feel claustrophobic or enclosed. The machine will make a whirring noise while you have the scan, and the whole process will usually be completed in less than five minutes. You will need to lie still while your body is scanned, and if the scan includes your chest you will be asked to hold your breath for ten seconds or so. Depending on the part of the body being scanned, you may be given some contrast medium which shows up on the scan and helps produce a sharper picture. Often, getting onto the couch and getting the contrast medium ready takes longer than the test itself. Here is one patient's experience.

❝ *I had some 'dye' injected to make things show up on the scanner; this was done through a needle in the back of my hand. One of the staff said it can make you feel a bit flushed and as if you've wet yourself, which I didn't believe until it felt just like that. I was very glad I'd been warned! You then lie down on a narrow bed and get pushed into the tube of the scanner, which can look a bit scary if you haven't seen one before. It would be a good idea to find out what it looks like beforehand. My scan was of my head, so going into the machine head first did feel a bit claustrophobic and it felt like it was taking quite a long time even though it was probably only a few minutes. The machine whirrs a bit while it's taking the scan. The staff have to leave the room to sit in a separate control room, so you do feel a bit all on your own, but there's a button you can press if you need help. I didn't need to use it, but it was nice knowing it was there.* **❞**

Magnetic resonance imaging (MRI) scans

This type of scan uses magnetic fields and radiowaves to produce detailed images of the inside of the body. It is often performed to look at the brain in a slightly different way to a CT scan, or to look at the ligaments and other soft tissues around joints such as the knee. Like a CT scan, it involves lying on a firm, narrow couch that moves in and out of a ring-shaped scanning machine. It makes more noise, and the machine itself is more like a tunnel than a doughnut, which can be a bit more uncomfortable for people who suffer from claustrophobia. MRI scans also take longer to perform, perhaps up to 30 minutes depending on what information is needed. You will generally be asked to lie as still as you can while being scanned.

The magnetic fields of the MRI scan exert a powerful attraction on some metal objects, which can be dangerous, so before you have an MRI scan there is a long checklist to fill out. Nearly all of the checklist concerns metal objects, such as pacemakers, implants and piercings, which are either inside someone's body or attached to it. Great care is taken to ensure no metal gets near the very strong magnetic pull of the MRI machine when it is active. If you are at all unsure about whether or not you can undergo an MRI scan because of a history of metalwork being placed in your body, make sure you ask the staff about it and get their advice.

Other radiology tests

There are many other tests that fall under the general umbrella of 'radiology'. Some are more specialist versions of those described above, such as X-rays combined with injecting or swallowing types of dye that show up on a dynamic (moving) X-ray. This is called 'fluoroscopy', and gives a picture which is more like a movie than a photograph. Others may be completely different, such as nuclear medicine tests, of which PET (positron emission tomography) scans and bone scans are some of the more common. While these may sound dramatic, they are done in a similar way to X-rays and involve using small doses of radioactive material to look at organs such as the lungs or thyroid gland.

Risks of radiology

The risks associated with any kind of radiological investigation are low and will be explained to you before you agree to have the test. You should ask the staff at any time if you have concerns, and you should also tell them if you have any allergies or other sensitivities.

Some people can have an allergic reaction to the 'contrast' used during scans. Many contrasts contain iodine as well as other chemicals, so you will be asked if you have any allergies beforehand. However, as with any substance, there is a small chance that you may have an allergic reaction after it is given even if you have never had it before or have never been allergic to anything in the past. Staff will monitor you to check for any kind of reaction. You should let them know if you feel unwell or notice any swelling or redness of your skin after having the contrast.

Many radiology tests, such as X-rays and CT scans, involve exposure to varying doses of radiation. Others, such as ultrasound and MRI, do not involve any radiation at all. The amount of radiation involved in individual tests varies. For example, a single X-ray of the chest is equivalent to roughly three days of background-level radiation that anybody encounters in day-to-day life outside the hospital. However, X-rays of other parts of the body and CT scans may involve significantly higher doses of radiation, equivalent to months' or years' worth of background radiation. A single CT scan of the abdomen, for instance, is equivalent to three years of background radiation, all on one day. The radiation dose involved is one of the factors that doctors will take in to account when suggesting that someone has a particular radiology test. It is also an important reason why doctors may avoid suggesting certain tests, or minimise their use, especially in certain groups of patients. For example, children and women of childbearing age seldom have CT scans if it can be avoided.

Endoscopy

An endoscope is a long, thin tube, a bit like a flexible telescope, which is used to look inside the body. Images of the inside of the body are relayed through the endoscope to a screen. The tube is usually flexible, but may sometimes be rigid, and is inserted through a natural hole in the body to allow the person performing the endoscopy to look directly inside. Endoscopy simply means all the tests in which an endoscope is used.

All forms of endoscopy use fibre-optic technology to allow the endoscopist to remotely inspect parts of the body. A light is shone down the endoscope to light up the inside of the body. Usually, the reflected light is then sent back and collected by a camera which displays it on a monitor. Some new endoscopes have a microchip at the end which collects the picture and then sends it digitally along the endoscope to a computer; the computer then decodes the picture for display on a monitor. The 'seeing' end of flexible endoscopes can be angled in different ways using controls at the 'operator' end, aiding careful inspection of your insides and also allowing delicate procedures to be performed.

Endoscopy is used to diagnose certain health problems that cannot be seen on radiological tests. It also allows the collection of small samples of tissue, which can then be looked at under a microscope to get more information about what may be wrong with you. An endoscope can also be used for certain forms of treatment, such as opening up a narrowing of the oesophagus (gullet), or removing small growths called polyps in the bowel or bladder.

Endoscopies are usually performed in special rooms where all the specialist equipment is set up, and there are usually dedicated members of staff, waiting areas and recovery areas. There are generally quite a few different members of staff, each with a specific job to perform. Typically members of the team include:

- *The endoscopist.* This is usually a doctor. It could be a consultant or a member of the medical team who is being trained or has completed training in the particular procedure. There are also an increasing number of specialist nurse endoscopists.
- *Nurses.* There are nearly always two nurses in any endoscopy room. Broadly speaking, one nurse will assist the endoscopist during the procedure and the other will help monitor you and talk to you during the procedure. This is usually very reassuring and calming and will distract you from the procedure.

Due to the nature of the test and the potential risks, you will be asked for your written consent before having one of these procedures. You should be given appropriate information and allowed the opportunity to ask questions before deciding whether you are happy to go ahead. Even if you decide to continue, you are still free to change your mind later and withdraw your consent – even during the procedure if you wish. The consent process is explained in more detail in Chapter 15, as it is an essential part of preparing for an operation or other procedure.

Some patients experience some discomfort during these procedures – which obviously varies depending on the patient and the specific test – but the vast majority of people tolerate endoscopy very well. The range of response is really wide; some patients undergo them with no sedation and no discomfort whatsoever, while others require much larger doses of sedation and pain relief. This is not a question of bravery – simply that for some people it appears very uncomfortable and for others it is relatively straightforward. You can always ask for sedation, even if it is not initially offered (which it may not be routinely for some endoscopic investigations, for example flexible sigmoidoscopy), but this is likely to mean that you need to be in the company of a responsible adult for the next 24 hours and that you cannot drive or operate heavy machinery for 48 hours.

Types of endoscopy

Endoscopy is carried out in different ways, depending on which part of the body is being examined:

Upper gastrointestinal (upper GI) endoscopy

This is one of the most common endoscopic tests. A flexible endoscope is inserted through the mouth, down the oesophagus (gullet) and into the stomach and the first part of the bowel. It is often referred to as a 'gastroscopy' or an 'OGD' (both of which refer to the parts of the body that it allows the doctor to study). Common reasons for this test being performed include symptoms suggesting a problem with the stomach or gullet – like acid reflux, difficulty or pain swallowing food – or unexplained weight loss or anaemia.

When you have an upper GI endoscopy, you effectively have to swallow the endoscope for it to pass down into your stomach. For this test, you will be asked not to eat or drink for six to eight hours beforehand to ensure your stomach is empty. A local anaesthetic will be sprayed on the back of your throat to reduce any discomfort from the endoscopy tube, and you wear a mouth guard to hold the endoscope away from your teeth. Swallowing the tube can be a little difficult, so you may be offered a sedative to help you relax, although you will still usually be awake throughout the procedure. Here is one patient's experience.

....

I was absolutely dreading having an endoscopy – I was worried that it would be difficult to swallow the endoscope tube and that it would make me retch. I'm a bit of a control freak and find anything like this really difficult. I explained these concerns to the doctor who was going to do the procedure and she was very reassuring. We agreed that I'd have some sedative medication as well as throat spray. She gave me the injection just before doing the procedure – and the next thing I remember is being in another room about half an hour later and it all being done. I honestly can't remember anything about it. Other than a slightly sore throat, I was completely fine, and I enjoyed a cup of tea and some biscuits before going home with a friend. If I ever have to have another one, I'll be a lot more relaxed about it!

Lower gastrointestinal (lower GI) endoscopy

There are two different types of lower gastrointestinal endoscopy – flexible sigmoidoscopy and colonoscopy. Both tests involve the endoscope being inserted through the anus (back passage) and into the colon. The two tests start the same way, but a colonoscopy passes through the entire colon and up into the final stage of the small bowel (called the ileum), whereas a flexible sigmoidoscopy is only used to assess the lower third to half of the colon (the bit nearest the patient's bottom). Common reasons for these tests being performed include symptoms suggestive of problems with the bowels – like bleeding from the bottom, difficulty with passing stools, weight loss, anaemia, or a strong family history of bowel cancer.

For a lower GI endoscopy, you will often also have some sedation and pain relief, particularly before a colonoscopy; this lasts longer and requires the endoscope to travel further inside you. You will also need to have some 'bowel preparation', to clean the colon so that the endoscopist can see. To empty the whole colon out normally takes about 48 hours of preparation beforehand, with your diet steadily decreasing from normal solids to clear liquids like water. It necessitates the taking of some very strong laxatives, which empty the bowel. If you are only undergoing a flexible sigmoidoscopy, though, you usually just have an enema into the rectum on arrival at the hospital; this empties out the bottom half of your colon just before the test.

Other types of endoscopy

A wide range of other endoscopic procedures can be performed. If there is a hole that allows access into the body, there is an instrument to look inside it! Other common forms of endoscopy include:

- *Bronchoscopy*. This involves looking through the mouth, down into the airways inside the lungs.
- *Cystoscopy*. This is used to look into the bladder via the urethra (the tube from the bladder to the outside of the body), which opens on the penis in men, and just above the vagina in women.
- *Nasendoscopy and laryngoscopy*. These involve looking inside the nose or mouth at the vocal cords, with the endoscope being inserted through one or other of the nostrils or the open mouth.

Risks of endoscopy

On the whole, endoscopic tests are incredibly safe. They are performed routinely in large numbers throughout the health service. However, inserting a flexible or rigid tube into a hollow part of the body inevitably involves a small risk of damaging the body and causing a hole. The risk is generally very low; for example, it happens to fewer than 1 in 1,000 people for an upper GI endoscopy or colonoscopy. With certain aspects of the treatment, or for individual patients, the risk of causing a hole may increase. This will be discussed with you in more detail before you are asked to provide consent for the procedure.

If the endoscope damages the wall of the part of the body being examined, or if a biopsy is taken, there may be some bleeding. This is usually minor and of no concern, but there is a small risk that more significant bleeding can occur, depending upon which test is performed and whether or not the endoscope is being used to provide any treatment at the same time. The risk of bleeding is increased slightly if patients take aspirin regularly, and increases more significantly if they take stronger anti-clotting medication such as warfarin or clopidogrel. For these reasons, you may be instructed to stop these medicines before your tests, but this will vary from patient to patient depending on the risks or benefits of doing so. Ask the doctors doing the test before changing any of your normal medication.

Significant complications as a result of endoscopy are very rare, and when they do occur they are usually recognised and resolved quickly. When you leave the endoscopy unit to go home, you will be given advice on what to look out for that may suggest a problem has developed after your test. In the vast majority of cases, any problems are dealt with at the time of the test or immediately afterwards.

If bleeding occurs, the most common approach to dealing with it is simply to monitor the patient carefully and see what happens. If necessary, the endoscopy can be repeated and techniques used via the endoscope to stop the bleeding, such as applying clips. Nearly always, this approach – perhaps with some medicines or blood products too – will stop the problem. If it does not, the next step is usually to ask the interventional radiologists to block the bleeding vessel by performing an angiogram (a special scan of the blood vessels) via a large vein or artery in the patient's groin. This is less invasive than a full operation and usually enough to deal with the problem.

If a perforation (a small hole) occurs, this can be a serious problem. Sometimes the body may heal itself, requiring nothing more than a period of close observation for the patient. If the problem does not settle down quickly, however, an operation may be required – but, to reiterate, this is a rare occurrence.

Treatment

CHAPTER FOURTEEN

Taking medication

Medication simply means the medicines or drugs used to treat or prevent illness. Many people take medication at home; this may be to treat an ongoing medical condition, to prevent one from occurring (for example, taking an aspirin a day to reduce the risk of a heart attack), or simply to relieve symptoms such as a headache or indigestion. Medication taken at home is usually in the form of tablets or a liquid, and may be prescribed by a doctor or bought 'over the counter' in a pharmacy or supermarket. Hospitals use many of these familiar drugs, but also provide a wider range, which are sometimes much stronger than those you might use at home. Drugs may also be given by other methods, such as an injection. This chapter describes how medication is used in hospital.

Preparing to go into hospital

If you take regular medication, it is a good idea to keep an up-to-date list of what you take and when. Doctors, dentists, opticians and many other health professionals will want to know what you are taking. It is useful to have this information available at all times, but particularly if you are about to go into hospital. Your personal list should include:

- any medication prescribed by your GP;
- any medication prescribed for you by a hospital clinic or other specialist clinic;
- any medication that you buy yourself from a pharmacy or supermarket;

- herbal, homeopathic, traditional or other complementary medicines that you use;
- creams, inhalers, skin patches and drops;
- any allergies or sensitivities to medication, foods or other things such as plasters.

The best way to keep a record of your medication is to write your own list that you update yourself, so that you can be absolutely sure that everything is correct. Some hospitals and clinics will give you a special booklet (a 'medication passport'), in which you can record the drug, the dose and the date you started the medication. There are also smartphone apps that you can use to record this information. A simpler alternative is to carry your 'repeat prescription request' list from your GP, if you have one. However, this will not include details of any specialist medicines that you get from a hospital or clinic, or anything that you buy yourself, so you may need to keep details of these as well.

The management of medication in hospital

The general process of admission to hospital has been described in Chapters 3–6, but it is useful to know how medication is managed in a little more detail. Your GP record contains your medication history, but in many areas of the country your GP records and your hospital records are not yet connected. This means that hospital staff do not generally know about your usual medication, and will have to ask you what you take. The best way for you to tell them is for you to show them your personal medication list, as described above. You may find that you are asked for this information several times. A doctor may ask for details of your medication, followed by a nurse, and then by a pharmacist who will check the details and make sure that you have supplies of everything you need. Being asked for information more than once can be irritating, but it allows hospital staff to check that they fully understand what medication you usually take. There are several reasons for this:

- Staff need to know what medication you usually take so that the correct drugs can be prescribed for you while you are in hospital.
- Doctors and pharmacists in the hospital need to check your current medication to see if any of it might be causing problems and might need to be changed.
- For some medical procedures, such as operations, some of your usual medication might need to be stopped or changed temporarily.
- Hospital staff will need to avoid prescribing any new medication that may interact with medication you take already.

Most hospitals ask you to bring in your own supplies of medication if you are being admitted to hospital, so that you can carry on taking the same medication as at home. Many ambulance services will also ask for your medication if they are collecting you from your home. If you have brought your own medication into hospital with you, a pharmacist or pharmacy technician will check it and will probably lock it into a medicine cabinet by your bed. If you have not brought in details of your own medication, the hospital staff can call your GP to find out what you are usually prescribed; this can sometimes delay your treatment, though, so it is better if you have the information with you.

When you are at home, your medication is prescribed for you by your GP. In hospital, however, everything has to be prescribed again by a hospital doctor or other registered prescriber, even if you have your own medication with you from home. This applies to all medication, including creams, inhalers and medication bought over the counter. This may seem a little 'over the top', but these additional checks help create as safe a process as possible and reduce the chance of any potentially serious errors.

In hospital your medication is recorded on a hospital medication chart. Traditionally this has been a paper chart kept at the end of your bed or in a folder at the nurses' station, but increasingly hospitals are using an electronic medication chart on a computer. Regardless of whether it is paper or electronic, the medication chart provides everyone with all the information about the medicines you are taking; the pharmacists know what medicine to supply, the nurses know what medication to administer, and all staff can check what medication you have been prescribed. You can look at your medication chart too. If you would like to do this, ask the pharmacist or nurse to show you and to explain the drugs and doses you have been prescribed. Box 14 suggests some other questions you may want to ask.

Box 14 *Questions to ask about medication*

- Have I been prescribed the same medication as I take at home?
- Have you changed any of my medication? If so, why?
- What is the medication for?
- Can I administer my medication myself?
- Are there any side-effects I should look out for?
- Is there any other medication I can ask for if I need it?

Taking medication in hospital

Most medication in hospital is administered by nurses in four daily medication rounds, typically around 8am, midday, 6pm and 10pm. During each of these rounds, a nurse will come to each patient in turn, check their medication chart, and administer any doses that are due. Medication can also be given at other times. For instance, you may be prescribed medication which is not given regularly, but which you can have when you, or a member of the nursing team, feel you require it. This is referred to frequently as 'PRN' medication, which stands for *pro re nata*, Latin for 'when required'. (As we have said before, old habits die hard in medicine!) Medication for pain, constipation and nausea is often prescribed to be given when required. Ask the nurse or pharmacist if you want to know what has been prescribed for you to take 'when required', and ask a nurse if you think you need it. Box 15 gives some tips on pain control.

Before giving you any medication, the nurse should check your identity, either by checking your hospital wristband or by

---

Box 15 *Helpful tips on pain control*

- Many people worry about being in pain, but nowadays it is almost always possible to control pain.

- If you are in pain, tell someone. Do not suffer in silence, as it is not helpful to your recovery.

- Pain medication is usually prescribed to be given regularly, with additional 'when required' doses which you can ask for between the regular doses.

- Do take pain medication that has been prescribed, even if you are not in pain. It is much easier to prevent pain than it is to control it once it starts.

- Sometimes more than one kind of pain medication is given, as they act in different ways and give a better effect when used together ('synergy').

- People sometimes worry about getting 'addicted' to pain medication. Most pain medication is not addictive, particularly if the medication is being used to treat or prevent actual pain. Speak to the doctor or pharmacist if you are concerned.

- Hospitals often have specialist 'pain teams' who can advise on pain medication for people with pain which is proving harder to treat.

asking you to state your name and date of birth. This can feel strange for both you and the nurse if you have been in hospital for a while, as the nurse probably knows very well who you are! However, it is important that this check always takes place to make sure that medication is given to the right person. In hospitals which use electronic medication trolleys, the checks may be done electronically; the nurse may scan a barcode on your wristband to confirm your identity, and in some cases may also scan each medication.

The medication you take in hospital may not look the same as the medication you take at home; the hospital pharmacy might use a different supplier. There is no need to worry about this, as you will be taking exactly the same drug – for example, paracetamol 500mg tablets will contain 500mg of paracetamol, regardless of who makes them or what they look like. But if you are not sure, always ask the nurse or pharmacist. Medication which is specifically for your use, and anything which you have brought in from home, will probably be kept in a lockable medication cabinet by your bed. These cabinets are sometimes called 'POD lockers'; POD stands for 'patients' own drugs'. Other medication may be stored in a medication trolley which the nurse wheels around the ward, or in a cupboard.

In many hospitals, 'self administration schemes' allow you to organise and take your own medication if you would like to, and if you are well enough. You may be asked if you would like to do this, but it is optional. If you would prefer the nurses to administer your medicines, you simply have to say so. If you would like to administer your own medicines but have not been invited to do so, ask a nurse or pharmacist if there is a scheme in the hospital. Many patients choose to administer their own familiar medication, but nursing staff will administer hospital-specific medication such as antibiotics and anything that must be given by injection.

Medication used frequently in the hospital

You are likely to be given new medication while you are in hospital, in addition to any medicines you usually take. There are many different types of medication, ways of giving it, and reasons for giving it. As well as specific medication given to treat your medical condition, common types of medication given in hospital include antibiotics, pain medication, symptomatic relief for problems such as constipation, and fluids given intravenously if you are not drinking normally. You are also very likely to be given an injection each day to prevent your blood clotting (see Chapter 20). For details on your specific drugs, ask your doctor, pharmacist or nurse.

Many hospital medicines are given as tablets or liquids in the same way as at home. However, for various reasons some drugs need to be given as injections or by other means. A common reason is that your healthcare team want the drug to act quickly, so an injection may be the preferred route of administration. Some drugs cannot be given by mouth, so another route has to be found:

Intravenous injections

Injections are given in various ways in hospital – most commonly into veins, muscles or areas of fat on the body. Intravenous injections (IVs) are given directly into a vein. There are several different types. 'Continuous infusions' are given over several hours or more, and usually involve a syringe or bag of fluid being given slowly via a pump. Other kinds of medication are given from a syringe into the bloodstream, over several minutes. In each case, the drug is introduced into the body through a vein, usually in the arm or hand, via a narrow flexible tube (a cannula) which can remain in place for a few days. We have described this in Chapter 9. The cannula only has to be put in once and then medication can be given when needed.

The doctor or nurse will find a suitable vein, use a tourniquet (a tight band around the arm) to make the vein stand out, and then use a hollow needle to introduce the tube into the vein. For children, a local anaesthetic cream is sometimes applied beforehand. The needle is then removed, leaving the soft, flexible tube in the vein, with a 'cap' to close it off when not in use. It can feel slightly uncomfortable as you move your arm around, or if you catch the cap on your clothing, but most people are hardly aware of it once it is in place. It is usually covered with a see-through dressing. If it starts getting painful, or red or swollen, or leaks blood or fluids, you should let your nurse or doctor know immediately. Most of the time these intravenous cannulas are changed every few days. If your cannula is not being used for anything, ask the nurse or doctor whether it can be removed.

Intramuscular injections

Often called 'IM' injections, these are medicines introduced directly into a muscle using a needle. The muscles of the leg or upper arm are most commonly used. The buttocks are the largest muscle in the body, so are sometimes used if a larger volume injection needs to be given. An intramuscular injection may be slightly uncomfortable; that depends on the medication being injected, how much of it is given and which muscle is used. However, any pain or discomfort is usually short-lived.

Subcutaneous injections

Often called 'sub-cut' injections, these are similar to intramuscular injections except that the medication is given into the layer of fat just under the skin. Again, it can be uncomfortable when the injection is given, but this only takes a few seconds. Insulin is typically given this way to people with diabetes.

Suppositories and enemas

Suppositories are waxy tablets and enemas are liquid medicines; both are inserted into your rectum (bottom). The enema pack usually has a short tube on the end, which is used to transfer the liquid. You may wonder why on earth you would ever need to do this! There are two main reasons. The first reason is that some medication used to treat the whole body is absorbed better or more quickly this way. The second is that some medication needs to be applied directly to the rectum to treat problems in this part of the body; problems include inflammation ('proctitis'), constipation and haemorrhoids ('piles'). Enemas are often used to empty the rectum by softening the stools and producing contractions of the bowels. This can be very helpful in constipation or if the bowel needs to be prepared for an endoscopic investigation (see Chapter 13).

When receiving a suppository or enema, you usually have to lie on your side. The nurse will wear gloves and place the suppository or enema tubing in using a finger and some lubricating jelly. It can feel a bit odd immediately after it has been inserted, and you will probably feel slightly uncomfortable for ten minutes or so after administration. A suppository then softens and melts and is absorbed with your body heat, and any discomfort wears off quickly. In the case of an enema, the liquid will often be designed to make you open your bowels shortly afterwards, so the enema liquid will be evacuated in this way.

Being discharged from hospital

Before you go home, a discharge prescription will be needed for any medication that you need to take with you. This is sometimes referred to as a TTA ('to take away') or TTO ('to take out'). It is ideally written a day or so before you go home, to allow the hospital pharmacy time to dispense any additional medication that you need and avoid any delays, although this is not always possible. If you brought in any of your own medication and it has not been used up, this should be given back to you.

Patients are usually given enough medication to last for at least a week after going home, but you may need to visit your GP to get a prescription for further supplies. You should also be given a copy of your discharge letter and prescription, which you can take to your GP and community pharmacist to help with arranging ongoing supplies, and to make sure that any changes made in hospital are updated on their records. The discharge prescription should tell you about any changes that have been made to your medication. Box 16 suggests some questions that you may want to ask about your medicines before you go home.

Box 16 *Questions to ask about medication before going home*

- Has my discharge prescription been written?
- Which medicines have been stopped/started/changed? Why?
- How do I get further supplies?
- Is there anything I need to look out for in terms of side-effects?
- What do I do if I have side-effects?

Medication safety and how you can contribute

Hospitals treat huge numbers of patients and use many different drugs. This can be a complicated process and sometimes mistakes occur. These can include some usual medication being missed off an inpatient prescription chart following admission to hospital, or the wrong type of medication being prescribed, or individual doses of medication being overlooked on the ward.

All staff involved with medication will be continually and conscientiously checking your medication, and there are various systems in place to prevent errors occurring. For example, some types of medication can only be prescribed by specialist doctors, and some drugs need to be checked by a second person before they can be given. This is also one of the reasons why you are likely to be asked for the same information more than once; a second person may pick up something that the first person has missed.

You and your family can also play an important role in checking medication, both in hospital and when you return home. When you are in hospital, you can make sure that hospital staff are aware of all the medication you were taking at home, how you were taking it, and any allergies that you have. When you are getting ready to go home, your role is to make sure you understand what medication you have been given and exactly when and how to take it. If it does not seem correct to you, or there is something you are not sure about, you or a family member must speak up and ask a nurse, doctor or pharmacist to check that everything is as it should be. Pharmacists focus specifically on medication and should be able to investigate, correct any problems quickly, and reassure you that all is well. So do ask to speak to the pharmacist allocated to your ward if you need to. Other tips, such as keeping an up-to-date list of your usual medication, and asking questions at each stage of your stay, have been highlighted earlier in this chapter. Remember that you are likely to know more about your own medication than anyone else. Your knowledge is, therefore, very important!

CHAPTER FIFTEEN

Having an operation

The development of safe anaesthesia and remarkable modern-day surgical techniques have transformed our lives. Many injuries and illnesses that would have been untreatable 50 or even 20 years ago are now managed safely and effectively, with operations considered as routine. The prospect of having surgery is a daunting one, though, even for those of us who have had an operation before. In consenting to have surgery, we are generally allowing someone to render us unconscious while another person alters, replaces, repairs or removes parts of our body.

Throughout this book we have emphasised that, as far as possible, you need to be active and enquiring. For most illnesses, people who take an active approach will adapt more easily and have better outcomes. When having surgery, though, we have to place ourselves completely in the hands of other people and trust that they will look after us. However important and confident we might be in daily life, we are suddenly vulnerable and may feel passive or rather helpless. The submission required to place ourselves 'under the knife' will for many of us be the most trusting thing we ever do. This may be hard to reconcile with the enquiring, balanced, equal relationship we advocate between you and your surgical team before and after the operation. If you are having surgery, it is important to accept that your role as a patient may be very different at different points in the surgical process. Before surgery, and when recovering afterwards, you should generally be as active, enquiring and participatory as possible, as there is much you can do to speed your recovery. However, during the operation and in the immediate recovery period you may need to just accept the process and allow others to look after you. We as authors speak from personal experience when we say that this can be a challenging thing to do.

When someone is asked to consent to surgery, the operation itself is usually described but the preparation and recovery periods can sometimes be overlooked by both the surgeon and the patient. We believe it helps to think of surgery as being the entire process from start to finish, rather than just the operation itself, although we recognise that the operation is the most significant aspect for most people. There are many things that need to be done both before and after the operation to make sure that you have a good outcome. People ask 'How long will the operation take?' but this does not really matter very much – your experience as a patient will be the same whether the answer is one hour or ten hours! The less frequently asked, but far more vital, question is 'How long will it take for me to get back to my normal life afterwards?'

This chapter describes the surgical process to help you know in advance what to expect. We also briefly describe different types of surgery. We cannot discuss all the different operations that are performed, and the ways in which your surgery will be tailored to your particular illness; your surgeon and other staff will discuss this with you. However, the broad process of surgery is similar for most operations.

Types of surgery

Surgery is used to treat an enormous range of conditions and covers everything from minor operations that may only take a few minutes to major operations that could last all day. Your surgeon and other members of the surgical team will explain the options available to you and the nature of any operation that you might have. In this section we explain the difference between open ('traditional') surgery and minimal access ('keyhole') surgery. We also describe newer techniques of interventional radiology which may be carried out by surgeons or by other doctors, and the use of various scanning techniques during surgery.

The majority of surgical operations, such as most hip or knee replacements, are planned in advance. This is better for the patient and for the staff, because just as for most things in life, preparation ensures the best outcome. However, sometimes surgery is needed as a matter of real urgency, such as for a hole in the stomach from an ulcer (not the sort of thing that can wait before being fixed!). The process described below relates to planned surgery, but emergency surgery follows essentially the same processes; the difference for the patient is that there may not be time for the full pre-operative preparation.

Open surgery

Open surgery is the traditional type of surgery, in which an incision (cut) is made for the surgeon to 'open' the joint, body cavity or area they are operating upon, in order to insert their hands and instruments. The surgeon is then able to directly see and feel the tissues that are being operated on.

Minimal access or 'keyhole' surgery

Minimal access surgery, commonly referred to as 'keyhole surgery', revolutionised modern surgical practice. Phenomenal technological advancements, particularly in the fields of lighting and optics, have allowed us to get better and better quality images from inside the body using smaller and smaller pieces of equipment. 'Thoracoscopic', 'laparoscopic', 'arthroscopic' and 'endoscopic' operations are all different variations on a theme; light sources and fibreoptic cameras allow surgeons to see and operate in places that previously needed very big incisions. Below, we describe an operation to repair an inguinal hernia, comparing the open and keyhole approaches.

A hernia occurs when an internal part of the body, such as a loop of bowel, pushes through a weakness in the muscle or other tissues to sit outside its normal cavity. An inguinal (pronounced 'ingwanal') hernia is one of the most common types, usually noticed as a swelling or lump in the groin. Surgeons can repair inguinal hernias either with the traditional open approach or using keyhole technology.

The open approach involves making a cut between 6cm and 10cm long. The surgeon cuts down to the hernia lump and 'reduces' it, placing it back in the abdomen. A mesh is placed over the weak spot where the hernia came through, to prevent it from returning. The surgeon then closes the incision with stitches or staples.

The keyhole approach is different. It involves a small incision made at the umbilicus (belly button), and the abdomen is inflated with carbon dioxide to make space to allow the surgeon to see. A camera with a light source, called a laparoscope, is placed in the abdomen and this relays images of the inside of the abdomen and pelvis to a television monitor. The surgeon can now see the hernia leaving the abdomen and going into the groin. A mesh is still placed, but on the inside of the hole, not the outside. The patient is left with a 1cm cut at the umbilicus and two 5mm cuts on the lower abdomen where the instruments were inserted. These are simply closed with stitches at the end of the operation, after the gas has been released, and small dressings are placed over the top.

People who have hernias on both their left and right sides can have both repaired at the same time, through those same small holes. People who are treated with keyhole rather than open surgery have less scarring, probably less pain, and a quicker recovery to full exercise and work. However, there are pros and cons to both approaches and it is therefore important to discuss these issues with your surgeon.

Interventional radiology

Interventional radiology is a rapidly growing specialty that uses imaging such as X-rays, ultrasound and computerised tomography (CT) scans to guide treatment. While these approaches are not usually described as surgery, the process as far as a patient is concerned is similar in some ways to a small operation. For example, you may well not be allowed to eat or drink anything beforehand, you may be anaesthetised (with a local or general anaesthetic) and you will sign a consent form. Many conditions that would previously have required a traditional operation can now be treated with these approaches. New imaging systems allow the radiology team to look inside your body and to follow the progress of their intervention very safely and precisely. These approaches can be used to open up blocked blood vessels (such as arteries and veins), to drain fluid, stop bleeding, treat some cancers, take biopsies from tissues, and for a variety of other medical purposes. Below is a description of a common type of interventional radiology procedure called an angioplasty.

....

An angioplasty is a way of relieving a narrowing or blockage in a blood vessel deep inside the body without having a full open operation. Angioplasty will usually be carried out in a special room in the cardiology or radiology department. The specialist doctors and the nurses will wear sterile gowns and gloves to carry out the procedure. You will be asked to get undressed and put on a hospital gown. You will then lie down and an X-ray machine will be positioned above you. The skin near the point of insertion, usually your groin or arm, will be swabbed with antiseptic and numbed with local anaesthetic.

A needle followed by a wire and catheter (a fine plastic tube) will be inserted into a major artery in your groin or arm. This 'access' allows the doctors to guide wires, balloons and stents (small tubes) through the arterial system to the problem area, guided all the time by inserting a special dye through the artery, which shows up on the X-rays. Once at the blockage, a special balloon is inserted, which is then inflated and deflated to widen the blockage, improving the flow through the blood vessel. To keep the artery open, a stent might be inserted and left in place to ensure the artery remains clear. The specialist will check the flow across the previously blocked area and, when satisfied that the artery is clear, will remove the equipment. All this happens inside your body, but the radiology team can follow the entire procedure on a screen using specialised X-ray equipment. An angioplasty generally takes about an hour and you can go home the same day.

....

Deciding whether an operation is right for you

There are three possible scenarios when considering an operation. First, there are occasions when surgeons are convinced that undergoing an operation is the right thing to do. In this scenario, the surgeon will probably say 'You really need this operation' or 'If you were my father/sister/child, I would be encouraging you to do this'. The surgeon should be able to quote clear figures and offer you studies or academic papers which have demonstrated clear benefits. For example, some cancers can be cured if the cancer is removed; if it is left inside the body, it will almost certainly be fatal. Another example of a highly recommended operation would be for a person whose eyesight has been severely diminished from cataracts; a straightforward operation can restore their vision.

The second scenario is more difficult for both the patient and the surgeon. This is when the surgeon suggests that the patient should not undergo surgery. The patient may understandably be desperate for a solution or an improvement. They may have heard of a procedure that they think will help. However, the surgeon may know that the operation is unlikely to help and might even make things worse. If a reputable surgeon says 'I would not currently operate on you', we recommend that you take this seriously. Most surgeons enjoy operating, so it is unlikely that their decision is being made through laziness or disinterest. Instead, this will be due to a belief that an operation will not help, or may make things worse.

The third scenario is the hardest, for both the patient and the surgeon, and involves uncertainty over the best course of action. This is something that some patients find hard to fathom. How can someone who has spent their adult life studying this specialty not know the best thing to do? But patients and their conditions are all different, and even if we can describe what happens to the 'typical' patient, there are still times when books, studies, science and long experience do not give a clear answer. In this case, a discussion about all the risks and all the potential benefits should take place. The surgeon will often try to gather more information, perhaps by performing other tests. They may ask for a second opinion from a colleague, or ask to discuss your situation at a team meeting. They may suggest that both you and they take some time to think about the best course of action. Time can often help a decision. Do not be disheartened or lose confidence in a surgeon who is willing to say that they cannot be certain about the outcome of surgery. We believe that they are often the good ones, as they do not have over-confidence in their own ability – nor do they have a disregard for the harm that surgery can cause if it is undertaken inappropriately. Box 17 suggests some questions that you may want to ask.

Consenting to an operation

If you decide that you wish to undergo an operation, you will be asked to 'consent' to it. This process is recorded by signing a consent form, written by the surgeon performing the operation or a member of their team. At the point of consent, the surgeon will tell you what the operation is, how it will be performed,

Box 17 *Questions you may want to ask your surgeon when considering an operation*

- What operation are you suggesting?
- What are the risks and benefits?
- What are the other options?
- What happens if I choose to do nothing?
- What kind of anaesthetic would I have?
- What kind of scar (if any) am I likely to have?
- What will be the long-lasting impact? Will I return to normal, or will I always be different in some way?

and what the benefits and risks are. They should also explain if there are other treatment options, such as physiotherapy, medication, or simply waiting to see if the symptoms resolve. They should tell you how many of these operations they have done previously, and what their results are like. They will tell you about, and document on the form, the name of the operation, any other specific interventions they wish to receive your consent for, and serious or frequent side-effects or complications. You may be given some written information during the consent process, and may be advised to visit certain websites or look up certain words or phrases. You may have questions (see Box 18). In non-emergencies you can always ask for some time to consider things, and an opportunity to return and discuss your options again.

Once you consent for the surgery to take place, your name will be added to the waiting list for the operation. The operation will take place very quickly if it is urgent, but there may be a wait for more routine treatment for longstanding conditions. The actual signing of the consent form can be carried out just before surgery, or consent can be given a few weeks beforehand in the clinic (if the surgery is planned in advance) and then just

---

Box 18 Questions you may want to ask after you have decided to have an operation

- Who will be involved and who will perform the operation?
- Where will the procedure take place?
- How long will I be in hospital – is it a day case or will I have to stay longer?
- How will the operation be done? What techniques will you use?
- What type of anaesthetic will be used – regional, local or general?
- When is the operation likely to take place?
- Do I need to stop eating or change my diet the day before the operation?
- Can I still take my tablets with water on the day of the operation?
- Are there any medicines that I should leave out before my surgery?
- Are there any extra medicines that I will need to take before surgery?
- Which ward or area will I go to afterwards?
- What kind of painkillers will I have afterwards?
- Will I have any extra tubes put in during the operation, such as a catheter or a drain?
- How long am I likely to take to recover?
- What should I do in terms of getting up and moving after the operation?
- Are there any restrictions to my work, driving or travelling afterwards?
- Will I need to have any stitches or clips removed after discharge. Who will do this?
- How will I bathe or shower after the operation? Should I cover the wound?
- Will I see you again at an outpatient appointment?

reconfirmed on the day. You should be offered a copy of your consent form to keep for reference.

How long will I be in hospital?

Most people now come into hospital on the day of their operation and stay there for much less time than they used to. After many minor procedures you can expect to go home the same day or the next morning. However, after major surgery you may be recovering in hospital for days or even weeks. You should be told in advance how long you are likely to stay in hospital, but remember that this is just a guide – everyone recovers at a different rate.

Preparing for surgery

While waiting for surgery, there are a number of things that you can do to improve your chance of the best possible outcome. First, and most important, stop smoking. Smoking damages your lungs and stops your blood from being able to carry oxygen effectively to the vital organs of your body. This is particularly unhelpful when your body is undergoing the stress of having an operation. If you stop even just a few hours before an operation, you can improve your chances of recovering well, as this will quite quickly improve your blood oxygen levels. If you do smoke, having surgery can often act as a trigger for you to stop smoking permanently, reducing your chances of getting lung cancer or having a heart attack, stroke or leg amputation in the future. Your GP or local pharmacist can give you advice and support to help you stop.

Second, if you are overweight, your surgeon may suggest that you try to lose some weight before the operation. In general, people of normal weight have fewer complications and a faster recovery than those who are overweight. Overweight people are more likely to have problems with breathing, post-operative mobilisation and infection. We cannot say for sure whether losing weight will be helpful in your particular case, but you should ask your surgeon for advice.

Finally, you must follow carefully any specific pre-operative instructions, particularly involving any medication you may already be on or be advised to start.

Pre-assessment clinic and pre-operative testing

For planned operations, you will nearly always be invited to attend a pre-operative assessment clinic before surgery. At this appointment you will probably meet with a specialist nurse or junior doctor who will ask you questions about your general health and examine you. The purpose of this visit is to make sure you are fit and ready for your operation. You may have some blood taken for tests, which will include checking your blood type in case you need a transfusion (see Chapter 16). If you have any personal or religious objections to blood transfusion, you should make them known so that appropriate arrangements can be made in advance. You will need to give full details of any medicines that you take and any allergies that you have, and highlight any particular dietary requirements. You can also discuss transport arrangements and any problems that you anticipate once you return home.

If you usually take medicines, you may be given specific instructions about these. Some medicines can complicate surgery by increasing the chances of bleeding and other problems. These include medicines that affect blood clotting, such as warfarin, aspirin, clopidogrel and dabigatran which many people take to prevent heart attacks and strokes. The pre-assessment clinic staff will tell you if you need to stop or change any of your medication; be sure to ask them if you are in any doubt about what you should do. Other replacement medicines may be given instead. For example, if you usually take warfarin, you may be prescribed a low molecular weight heparin instead, which is a shorter-acting medication given by injection under the skin. Other medicines may also need to be stopped a few days before your operation. You will be told which medicines to take on the day of surgery and which to leave out. For example, if you take the diabetic medicine metformin, you will probably be asked to stop taking this a few days before your operation. If you inject insulin, you may be asked to come into hospital the day before surgery so that your blood sugar levels can be monitored while you are not eating, and an insulin infusion can be set up if required. There may be other specific things you need to do in the final few days before your operation, such as 'bowel preparation', which means taking strong laxatives to empty your bowels before surgery in that part of your body.

Particularly before a major operation, the medical team may decide that they need to carry out further tests. For instance, they may need to check how well your heart and lungs are working, or find out if you have any other medical problems. These tests will be arranged for you, but it can take a few days or weeks for them to be carried out, which may mean delaying the date of your operation. Although this can feel frustrating, this preparation is in your best interests and will help ensure that the surgery is performed as safely as possible.

Final preparations before coming into hospital

You will be given a date and a specific time to come into hospital, and instructions about where to go. This usually means arriving on the morning of surgery, although some people are asked to come in a day or so beforehand. You will usually be asked to fast (stop eating) for some hours before the operation. This is so that your stomach is empty, which reduces the risk of vomiting while you are anaesthetised. You should be allowed to drink water until just a couple of hours beforehand and, increasingly, 'enhanced recovery' programmes are allowing patients to take specific pre-operative nutritious drinks until a few hours before surgery. Ask about these possibilities, and follow the advice that the surgical and anaesthetic teams give.

Even when fasting, you can usually take tablets with a small amount of water on the morning of surgery, but you should check with your doctor first. You may also be asked to take a shower on the morning of surgery, with an antibacterial soap, to reduce the risk of getting an infection in your wounds after the operation.

After arriving at the hospital and 'checking in', you will probably receive visits from members of the surgical and anaesthetic teams. The surgeon will talk to you about the operation and discuss the risks and benefits. At this point you should ask any remaining questions that you may have. Once you have agreed to go ahead, you will be asked to sign a consent form, as described above, or confirm the consent that you previously gave in the outpatient clinic. The surgeon may draw a temporary mark on your skin to identify the side of the surgery. If the scar is going to be in a hairy area, you may also need to have the hair shaved beforehand, although this is often done after the anaesthetic has been administered, in the operating theatre. The anaesthetist will see you separately and ask some specific questions that help them to plan for the procedure. They may also perform a short examination and explain the type of anaesthetic that they will use.

Your experience of the operation

A patient's experience of a surgical operation depends to a large extent on the type of anaesthesia they have. While there are many types of anaesthetic, the three main categories are general anaesthesia (GA), local anaesthesia (LA) or regional anaesthesia (often referred to as 'epidurals', 'spinals', 'caudals' or 'nerve blocks'). Some patients have a combination of different types of anaesthesia; for example, a general anaesthetic and an additional regional anaesthetic for pain relief after the operation.

General anaesthesia

If you are given a general anaesthetic, you will be completely unconscious ('asleep') throughout the operation. The anaesthetic is usually administered in a special anaesthetic room next to the operating theatre. You will lie on a trolley in the anaesthetic room and a cannula will be put into a vein, usually in your arm or hand. You may be given some oxygen to breathe through a mask, and then medicines will be injected into the vein. You will find that you suddenly feel extremely tired, and that will be the last thing you know until you come round in the recovery room or ward. From the time when you fall asleep in the anaesthetic room, you will not feel or remember anything until the anaesthetic is stopped at the end of the operation, after which you will gradually wake up. The experience feels the same whether your anaesthetic lasts for 15 minutes or 15 hours – all sense of time disappears. After you fall asleep, the anaesthetist will put a soft plastic tube through your mouth and into your lungs to allow the passage of air, oxygen and anaesthetic gases into your lungs, and will continue to make sure that you are comfortable and safe during the procedure. You might notice a slightly sore throat after the operation; this is due to the breathing tube and wears off within a few days. Here is one patient's experience.

....

I was quite daunted about having my first general anaesthetic, but the anaesthetist made me feel very relaxed while he was getting everything ready in the anaesthetic room, chatting about what I did for a living. He put a cannula in my hand and then explained about the medicines he was injecting.

There was an anti-sickness drug, then a strong painkiller which made me feel rather lightheaded and giggly. He then started injecting the anaesthetic drug and I must have fallen asleep after about two seconds as the next thing I remember was waking up in the recovery room and realising it was all done. I had no sense of anything that happened in between or how long it took, which felt rather strange – like some kind of black hole! I went home a few hours later, after a nice cup of tea, and enjoyed having a meal because I hadn't eaten all day.

....

Local anaesthesia

Local anaesthesia involves the injection of a numbing medicine through the skin around the area where the operation is taking place. You may well have had a local anaesthetic injected into your gums during a visit to the dentist before a tooth was filled or removed.

If an operation is performed solely with local anaesthetic, you will be awake and conscious throughout. You will first feel a small needle being inserted into the skin, and then a stinging sensation as the anaesthetic is injected. It is a bit like being stung by a bee! After a few minutes the area will be completely numb to pain, although you may be able to sense if the surgeon is pushing or moving the skin or tissues. If you begin to feel pain during the surgery, you should say so; additional local anaesthetic will be administered. Common procedures done in this way include removing small skin lesions such as cysts or moles, or the removal of ingrowing toenails. During larger operations the surgeon will often infiltrate the wounds being made with local anaesthetic even though you are fast asleep, so that when you wake up the wounds are numb for the first 12–24 hours. This helps you get up and move around more quickly. Here, a patient describes his experience of having a minor operation.

....

❝ *I had a 'venous malformation', a little blue blob, on my lip, which was slowly getting bigger and becoming unsightly. I saw a plastic surgeon, who said he could remove it under local anaesthetic, injected just beforehand. I was nervous, as I hadn't had an operation done this way before, but also pleased – he said I'd be able to walk straight out of the operating theatre and home afterwards, and I didn't want to take any time off work.*

I lay on the operating table and the local anaesthetic was injected into my bottom lip. This hurt and made my eyes water – I could feel the needle going in and the fluid being injected. It didn't last long, though, and about two minutes later he said he was about to start and to let him know if I had any pain. I couldn't feel a thing! All I could feel was a bit of pulling as if someone was gently tugging on my lip. This was remarkable, because I could see him, his hands and the instruments, and I could hear the beeping of a machine.

The whole thing, including the stitches, took about ten minutes. Afterwards my lip felt like it almost didn't belong to me and it was difficult to drink a cup of tea. This slowly wore off, though, after about six hours. Apart from feeling a bit sore – like I'd been punched in the mouth – for a few days, there were no other effects. If possible, I'd really recommend surgery under local anaesthetic. All the times I've had general anaesthetic I've felt groggy and tired for a few days afterwards. But on this occasion I felt like normal and was able to work and exercise. I'm also glad I had it done – my lip looks perfect now, with just the tiniest of scars. ❞

....

Regional anaesthesia

A regional anaesthetic is similar to a local anaesthetic in that it involves similar numbing agents. However, regional anaesthesia differs from local anaesthesia in that much larger areas of the body, such as an entire limb, are numbed by injecting anaesthetic around the nerve or nerves that carry sensation from that part of the body back to the brain.

Epidural or spinal anaesthetic is a common type of regional anaesthesia, used during childbirth and for some surgical operations. This type of anaesthesia numbs the whole lower half of the body. With an epidural anaesthetic, an extremely thin plastic tube will be put into your back. This tube will be connected to a pump that steadily provides the numbing drugs to the area. If necessary, the tube can be left in place for three to four days and additional drugs can be given to provide continued pain relief after the operation. This can be very useful for big operations, because your need for other painkiller tablets or injections afterwards is usually reduced. However, epidural and spinal anaesthetics can make it more difficult for you to stand and walk until they wear off, and you may temporarily need a catheter (a tube in the bladder) to pass urine, because sensation to the bladder is lost until the effects of the anaesthetic wear off. This patient had abdominal surgery with a spinal block.

....

▌▌ *This was definitely a very strange experience. For one thing, I walked into the operating theatre, which is a place you don't usually get to see as a patient. The operating table was very narrow, more like a shelf than a bed. Having a spinal block involves a small tube being inserted into your spine – they wipe your back with disinfectant and then you have to curl over so that the anaesthetist can get a needle in between the vertebrae. It's a bit uncomfortable, but not really painful. Then they take out the needle, but leave behind a little tube which the anaesthetic is fed into. Your lower body starts to go completely numb, so you can't move, can't feel anything, and I was worried I'd roll off this narrow little table, which of course I didn't. I was also a bit worried that they might start the operation before the anaesthetic* *had worked properly, but they tested it thoroughly by spraying cold stuff on my body and checking I couldn't feel anything.*

You have to wear various monitors, and they put a drape across my chest so that I couldn't see what they were doing, which I was pleased about as I didn't feel any need to see what my insides look like! The anaesthetist was next to me, and kept talking to me, and we had the radio on. When the surgeon started cutting, I could feel things being really tugged around inside my belly, but no pain whatsoever. I think this in itself was rather confusing – I felt as though part of me was saying 'help, this is really going to hurt' and another part of me was saying 'but it doesn't, so relax...'. It's like having dental work done with a very good local anaesthetic, but on a bigger scale. 🎧

If you are awake during an operation performed using local or regional anaesthetic, you will be able to hear, see and smell what is going on around you. This may include hearing music being played in the operating theatre, and/or the staff talking to each other. You will not normally be able to see the wound during the operation, as a drape will be positioned to prevent this. You will, of course, be able to talk to the staff, who can tell you about the progress of the operation and reassure you if you are worried about what is happening. You may be given a little bit of sedation, just to reduce the natural anxiety one feels when undergoing an operation.

What happens while I am anaesthetised and asleep?

Once you are asleep, a number of further procedures will be carried out before your operation starts. You will usually not be aware of any of these, but we thought we would share them with you so you have an idea of what will happen.

You will be gently lifted onto the operating table and positioned appropriately. Not all operations are performed with the patient lying flat on their back. Sometimes patients are sitting up (for example, for shoulder operations); sometimes they have their legs up in stirrups (for example, for operations on the pelvic organs); and sometimes they are lying on their stomach (for example, for operations on the spine) or on their side (for operations on the aorta, the biggest artery in the body, for example). There are many other positions that may be used. You need to be positioned and secured safely. You will probably also have calf compressors attached to your calves, to keep blood pumping out of your (now stationary) legs; this helps prevent clots in the veins. You may have a urinary catheter placed at this point, and any other drips or cannulas. Hair will be removed from the operation site if necessary.

When everything is ready, but before the cleaning and draping of the area to be operated on is performed, the World Health Organization Checklist will be performed. This process, introduced into hospitals around 2008, is an important safety mechanism and requires all the staff in the operating theatre to pause, and to run through a series of important checks. These include checking who you are, what operation is to be done, what equipment is required and that it is present and working correctly, and what special medication or needs you may have during the procedure. Think of this as a 'pre-flight check', similar to those that are performed on every aeroplane and in every cockpit around the world before take-off. There is clear evidence that it helps prevent errors and also improves team morale and interaction.

Once everybody is happy to proceed, the surgeons and the theatre nurse will 'scrub up' and will begin the case. There is no 'generic' operation to describe at this point; some operations are routine, some are incredibly challenging. Surgeons perform operations for all sorts of reasons: to repair broken or damaged tissues, to improve function, to stop bleeding, to remove cancers, to drain pus and to remove blockages. They operate on every single part of the body, from the brain or inner ear to the inside of the heart and the sole of the foot. When your particular operation is finished, you will be slowly taken off the operating table and transferred to a bed.

After the operation

After the operation has finished, you will normally be taken to a recovery area where a nurse will monitor you and perhaps one or two other patients who have had operations. If you have had a general anaesthetic, you may sometimes be woken up in the operating theatre first to make sure you are coming round normally. However, your memories of this are likely to be slightly blurred due to the effect of the anaesthetic and you will probably only really be aware of what is going on around you after you get to the recovery area. When you are fully recovered from the anaesthetic, you will be taken back to the ward – or, in the case of very major operations, to intensive care or a specialised post-operative high dependency unit. In the event of day-case surgery, you will be allowed to go home accompanied by a responsible adult, normally after you have had something to eat and drink and have passed urine.

In the immediate post-operative phase, you may begin to feel some soreness or nausea as a result of the surgery or medication. If this happens, you should tell the nursing staff so that you can be given some painkillers or anti-sickness medication. Note that your family or friends may not be allowed to visit you immediately, while you are being closely monitored to make sure you are recovering as expected.

After major operations you may wake up in an intensive care unit or high dependency unit. You will usually be told about this possibility beforehand. In this case, you may find that you are attached to some tubes. For example, you may have tubes inserted into the veins of your neck, through your nose to your stomach, or in your bladder to drain urine. There may be drains in cavities such as your abdomen or chest to remove fluid or blood. You will have been told about these tubes when you agreed to the operation, and the surgeon will have explained if it is a standard part of the procedure. Intensive care is described in more detail in Chapter 9.

Recovery and preparing to go home

Below are a surgeon's and a patient's perspectives on the recovery process. Major surgery is done in a calm, methodical and careful manner, but your body experiences it as a major trauma. Your body reacts to surgery in the same way as to a major injury, by releasing all its stress hormones and protective chemicals into the blood, shutting some processes down and focusing all its energy on rebuilding and recovering. Imagine that you have

....

Having an operation is a controlled trauma, and yet patients' expectations of recovery can sometimes be wildly optimistic. I've looked after patients who, two weeks on from a four-hour anaesthetic and major bowel removal, are surprised that they still feel somewhat tired – but I'm always convinced that if they'd been hit by a bus two weeks earlier, they'd be astonished by how well they were doing! Recovery after surgery is usually quite quick at first and then slower – you recover most of your normal functions really rapidly, but the body continues to heal and improve months afterwards. Most patients I've cared for who have undergone major surgery report ongoing improvement as much as a year after surgery, so I urge patients not to be disheartened if a month afterwards they still don't feel quite themselves. Time remains the best healer of all.

....

been in a major traffic accident; even if you have not suffered any major injuries, you would expect that it would take some time to recover from the shock. It also takes time to recover from surgery; you should expect this and be prepared for it.

Do not worry if it takes some time before you start to feel like your normal self. You may initially not have enough energy to get out of bed and move around without help and support. For some operations, particularly spinal and orthopaedic (bone and joint) surgery, you may be kept in bed for a short period after the operation. In general, though, you will be asked to get

....

" *The thing that took me by surprise when I had my operation was that it was an emotional rollercoaster as much as a physical one. I was prepared for some pain or discomfort afterwards, but not for the emotional aspects of recovery. Beforehand, there was some anxiety about the operation and the anaesthetic, as well as some excitement about finally getting a longstanding problem sorted out. Then I remember the anaesthetist injecting the anaesthetic drugs into a tube on the back of my hand, and feeling very happy and giggly.*

I woke up some time later feeling a bit shivery and disorientated, breathing oxygen through a mask and wanting to cry. This was then followed by a bit of a 'high' – probably a mixture of relief that it had all gone OK and the effects of the pain medicines. I ended up (rather manically) phoning all my friends and family to tell them I'd had the operation and it was all fine, and wanting to hug all the staff. But this was followed by feeling quite depressed and very emotional for a few days once the initial euphoria wore off, things starting to hurt, feeling really tired, and the realisation that it was going to take a while to properly recover. I suppose it's good to realise that your body goes through quite a lot when it's operated on, and you just need to take the necessary time to recover. **"**

....

up and about as soon as possible (even if you do not feel like it!). Your rehabilitation may include a visit from the physiotherapy team, who will get you moving and instruct you on exercises to speed up your recovery. Moving about can be very beneficial, as it reduces your risk of infections and blood clots and stops you from losing muscle strength. It also helps you breathe better, increasing the amount of oxygen in your lungs and preventing chest infections.

You should have little or no pain or sickness after the operation. The doctors and nurses will try to prevent them by giving you a variety of painkillers and anti-sickness medication. These are most commonly given in the form of tablets or injections. However, for larger operations a portable machine called a PCA (patient-controlled analgesia) pump may be set up, which allows you to press a button and receive a dose of painkiller on demand. PCA pumps are safe because they are programmed to prevent you from receiving an overdose; they are also convenient because you can press the button whenever your pain might increase, such as when you want to move around in bed. They leave you in control and not as dependent on others for your pain relief. Most patients find this very reassuring. Finally, if you have any tubes such as drains, catheters and drips, these will be removed one by one during the course of your recovery. Occasionally, patients go home with these in place, but your medical team will let you know if this will be the case.

Discharge and follow-up

Once you have recovered enough from your operation, you will be discharged with a plan in place for your ongoing care. This will often include a follow-up clinic appointment with the surgeon, although for more minor procedures this is not always necessary – after removal of your appendix or repair of a simple hernia, for example, your GP can check on your recovery. The general process of leaving hospital is described more fully in Chapter 26, but there are some points which are particularly important for patients who have had surgery.

After surgery many people are eager to leave hospital as soon as possible and recover in the familiarity and comfort of their own homes. Others, perhaps still feeling frail and vulnerable, feel safer in hospital. Patients and families sometimes believe that they are being hurried to leave because the hospital 'needs the beds'. While there is sometimes a pressure on beds, this is very seldom the reason that surgeons want to discharge patients. People used to be kept in hospital for days or even weeks, but it is now known that people recover much more quickly and are generally safer at home. Most people will eat and sleep better at home, can wash and bathe more easily, can see their friends and family, can exercise whenever they want to, and are much less vulnerable to infections than in hospitals. In terms of workload, it makes little difference to hospital staff which patient is in the bed, so any desire to get you home is based on your best interests and not on any 'need for a bed'.

You should be given specific instructions regarding wounds at the time you leave hospital. Many skin stitches dissolve by themselves over time, but you will be told if someone needs to physically remove them. This can usually be performed by a nurse in your local GP practice, or by a district nurse in your home if you are unable to go to your local health centre or GP practice. More complicated wound-care arrangements will be discussed with you if necessary. You should also ask the surgical team about showering and bathing, to see if they advise that the wound should be covered or if you should avoid it getting wet. In general, though, wounds should not be soaked for the first two weeks, but can get wet in the shower. They should then be patted dry or dried carefully with a cool hairdryer. A fresh dressing can be applied if the previous one has come loose.

When you get home, you may find that you are more tired than usual, and occasionally your memory and thinking may be slightly impaired. This 'hangover' effect is common. Some people find that they are rather emotional and tearful on the second day after a general anaesthetic. This is a temporary effect of the anaesthetic and other medicines, and should wear off fairly quickly. Depending on the operation you have undergone and your occupation, you may need to get specific advice regarding your ability to work, drive and travel. You should not drive or operate any machinery while taking strong painkillers. If you need to drive soon after a major operation, you can discuss this with your surgeon and the team of doctors looking after you. You may wish to check with your insurance company to make sure you are appropriately covered. Remember, though, that the legal requirement to be safe to drive remains with you; you have to be safe to perform an emergency stop, and the rest is just advice or guidance. No doctor can 'clear you' to drive.

CHAPTER SIXTEEN

Receiving a blood transfusion

The average adult human has around five litres of blood flowing around their body at any given time; the exact amount depends on weight, height and gender. Blood is a mixture of important cells (red blood cells, white blood cells and platelets) and a solution called 'plasma', which is made up of water, proteins and salts. This amazing concoction does all sorts of jobs, carrying oxygen and vital supplies to the tissues, bringing waste products back, and helping you fight infection.

Giving blood to someone to support their recovery from an illness or injury is called 'blood transfusion'. A patient may be given a blood transfusion because for some reason they are unable to maintain the correct balance of cells and proteins in their blood. This may be due to bleeding, destruction of blood cells within the body, or an inability to make new blood components as the current ones wear out. Blood transfusion can be life-saving, particularly when someone is bleeding heavily and their body cannot make new blood quickly enough to replace it.

Blood transfusion is a very safe process and relatively common in modern medicine. However, as with most medical treatments, there are always some risks. Doctors will therefore try to use simpler treatments and only transfuse blood when absolutely necessary. This chapter focuses on giving blood transfusions to adults, and explains what is involved.

Blood donation and blood groups

The NHS is very fortunate in having a system of voluntary blood donation. Many of us spend an hour every few months giving blood that will later be used to help other people. However, you cannot simply take blood from one person and give it to another, because there are different types of blood known as 'blood groups'. Each blood group is only compatible with some of the other blood groups, so any unit of blood has to be 'matched' with the blood of the potential recipient before it can be transfused. If the wrong kind of blood is given to someone, it can make them very sick.

When blood is donated, it is first processed and separated into many useful components: red blood cells (commonly referred to as 'packed red cells'), plasma, platelets and clotting factors. Each different part of the blood can then be given to patients who need that specific part, so one donated unit of blood may be used to help several patients. When people talk about 'having a blood transfusion' or 'being given blood', they are usually receiving 'packed red cells', but to keep it simple we will continue to refer to it as 'blood'. The other constituent parts are more specialised, and are given to people with more specific medical problems; we will not focus on them here.

Reasons for blood transfusion

Red blood cells carry oxygen to the tissues of your body using an important molecule called haemoglobin, which carries the oxygen within the cell. If the amount of haemoglobin in your blood drops below its usual level, you are described as being 'anaemic'. If the level of haemoglobin falls significantly, the tissues of the body may not receive enough oxygen and so cannot work properly. This can make you ill.

Anaemia may occur because the body is not making enough haemoglobin, because the haemoglobin is faulty, or because a person has lost a lot of blood. Common causes of anaemia include deficiencies of iron, vitamin B12 or folate (all of which are essential for making haemoglobin), chronic blood loss in women who suffer very heavy periods, sickle cell disease (in which the haemoglobin is faulty), and blood loss during and after surgery. Anaemia often develops slowly over weeks or months. Many people can suffer from mild anaemia and not experience any symptoms at all, as the body can compensate quite well up to a certain point. However, once anaemia becomes more serious they may have symptoms such as profound tiredness, breathlessness, chest pain and palpitations. In these circumstances, it is important to correct the anaemia quickly. Sometimes this can be done by replacing the deficient vitamins or minerals that may have caused the anaemia, such as by giving iron tablets or injections. However, it may be necessary to correct the problem more rapidly by transfusing blood. In general, only enough blood is given to correct the immediate symptoms and allow the body to function normally. The underlying problem is then addressed with the aim of avoiding any further transfusions.

How is a blood transfusion given?

If your doctors think you might need blood at some point in your hospital stay, they will send a small sample of your blood to the blood transfusion laboratory. This is commonly known as a 'group and save', because the laboratory technicians do just that; they work out what your blood group is and then save the rest of the sample in case it is required for a second check. If you then actually need a transfusion, a 'cross-match' can be performed, either on the saved sample or on a second blood sample, depending on local policy. When a cross-match is performed, the actual blood to be transfused is tested against your blood to get a very detailed compatibility check. On occasion, further checks and investigations may be required, as some people have very unusual blood types. Once the laboratory is satisfied, they will label a unit of blood specifically for you.

If you have previously had a blood transfusion, even if this was a long time ago or at another hospital, it is important to mention this to the staff looking after you. Also, if you have ever been given a card stating that you have specific needs in relation to blood, be sure to show the staff this card or tell them about it. This can speed up the identification of suitable blood which is safe for you to receive, and prevent any delay to your blood transfusion or other operations or procedures.

Once blood has been prescribed for you, and the laboratory has successfully cross-matched a unit or more of blood for you, it is brought from the blood bank to the ward or operating theatre by specially trained blood bank porters. The staff looking after you will then carry out a series of further identification checks to confirm that the blood matches your name and prescription. You will be asked to confirm your identity by stating your name and date of birth. The clinical team will also check your wrist-band to ensure that the hospital number matches the one on the blood bag. These are very important checks and patients can sometimes be bemused by the process, particularly if they have been an inpatient on the ward for a long time and think all the nursing staff will know them. However, patients on the ward may have identical or similar names and birthdays, and mistakes can have very serious consequences, so these checks are done with every transfused unit of blood. If you require blood and are anaesthetised, or are too unwell to confirm your own identity, the team will carry out these checks against your wristband.

Each unit of blood is stored in a special plastic bag and is chilled. Once all checks have been carried out, the blood is transfused through a drip into a vein, normally over several hours. If required, it can be delivered into the body very rapidly indeed, but this only tends to be done if someone is losing a lot of blood.

If you are having a transfusion, you do not need to do anything except lie or sit still while the blood is slowly introduced into your blood stream. The nursing staff will keep you under close observation during the transfusion, and will carry out regular monitoring of your temperature, pulse and blood pressure. To ensure blood is given safely, and that the required observations do not disturb your sleep, blood is usually transfused during the day rather than at night unless absolutely necessary.

How will I feel during the transfusion?

Most people feel fine during a blood transfusion. Some people will experience mild temperature changes, chills or a rash, which can easily be treated with paracetamol or by slowing down the speed of the transfusion. However, if you feel unwell or experience any symptoms beyond these, you must tell the nursing or medical staff immediately. Very occasionally, the transfusion may have to be stopped and patients may be unable to receive the whole unit of blood because of an adverse reaction. Severe and unexpected reactions are very rare indeed, but hospital staff are trained to recognise complications from blood transfusion and how to manage them.

Will I need a transfusion during my operation?

The vast majority of people undergoing an operation do not require a blood transfusion. Modern surgery has become far more adept at preventing blood loss, and despite what you may see on the television, most operations involve little blood loss – even really major procedures. However, for some operations the surgeons will want to have blood on standby just in case it is needed.

Some people have an increased risk of bleeding, even in routine operations. This may be due to a genetic disposition, because of an illness, or because they have to take 'blood-thinning' medicine (such as aspirin, clopidogrel or warfarin). Checking for any disposition to bleeding is an important part of the routine pre-operative assessment process. Any patient taking blood-thinning medication may be advised to stop taking this before surgery, if it is safe to do so, or they may be admitted to hospital slightly ahead of their procedure to allow the team to alter their medication.

Most blood transfusions required during an operation can be predicted in advance by the surgical team looking after you. If this is the case, you will be asked to consent to a possible transfusion before the operation takes place. If you have a religious (or other) objection to blood transfusion, you should discuss this with your surgeon before the operation, and if at all possible before your admission to hospital. This will allow the clinical team to assess the risks of bleeding and make alternative plans. Some surgical departments use 'cell salvage' during an operation, which is a means of recycling your own blood. This is not suitable for all operations, but do ask your surgical team if it is an option in your case.

It is best to have a normal haemoglobin level before an operation in order to reduce your chances of requiring a blood transfusion. If you are anaemic, the cause will be investigated and you may be prescribed iron tablets to take for a month or so before an operation, or even given a blood transfusion in advance of the operation.

Having regular blood transfusions

Some people require regular blood transfusions. While the principles of the matching process remain the same, the process can be slightly more complicated; their blood is likely to have special requirements. If you have frequent transfusions, your body may make antibodies against other people's blood even if you have been closely cross-matched each time. If you receive blood regularly, the samples you provide for the blood bank must also be timed as close as possible to the planned transfusion (usually no more than 24 hours in advance of the transfusion). Sometimes this involves special blood units being sent from the regional Blood and Transplant Service by car or motorcycle courier.

Having regular blood transfusions can therefore be a lengthy process and involve a lot of time waiting for the next step. The clinical team will appreciate that waiting is very frustrating, and services have become more efficient and more patient-centred than they used to be. If you attend hospital regularly, there may also be other options to make things easier for you. For example, if you live nearby you might prefer to attend the day before for your cross-match blood test and return the next day, or perhaps go home after your cross-match and ask to be telephoned to come back when the blood transfusion is ready.

Is blood safe?

Although the process of blood transfusion has many steps and there is a small risk of an error at each one of the steps, the highest risk is that blood intended for one patient is accidentally given to another. Overall, however, the process is extremely safe.

In recent years blood transfusion risk-management programmes have been implemented in UK hospitals. These include all the identity-checking processes described above. Some hospitals now have electronic checks and bar-coding systems. All staff involved in any step of blood transfusion processes are also carefully trained, and assessed regularly. The most important thing that you can do is to cooperate with the repeated checks, as these are designed to protect you. You should speak up immediately if you think there is any confusion about your name, or if a staff member does not check your identity at any stage of the process.

Is there a risk of infection from blood?

In the UK, all blood donors are unpaid and the UK Blood and Transplant Service uses comprehensive pre-donation question-naires to prevent donations from anyone thought to be at risk of a transmissible infectious disease. Only donors who have 'passed' the questionnaire are able to give blood, and even then every sin-gle donation is screened for a wide variety of infectious diseases (including viruses such as hepatitis B, hepatitis C and HIV). The technology for screening blood donations for infectious agents has improved significantly over the last decade, and infections can now be detected at very low levels indeed. Any blood that is detected as being infected is discarded; the donors are informed and prevented from giving further donations. There have been no cases of transmission of hepatitis or HIV through blood trans-fusion for over ten years now in the NHS, even though millions of transfusions have taken place during that time.

The risks of infection from blood are therefore very low indeed. However, there is always some risk associated with trans-fusion and it is possible that there could be other risks in the future, such as from new infectious diseases. For these reasons, blood transfusion is only carried out when absolutely necessary.

Can my relatives or friends donate blood to me?

People sometimes ask if they can receive blood from one of their relatives. Blood donations from relatives or friends are known as 'directed donations'. However, the UK Blood and Transplant Ser-vice discourages the use of directed donations and this approach is not recommended by any European blood service. There are several reasons for this. Blood donations need to be carefully matched for blood group and antibodies, and there is no guaran-tee that a relative's blood is any more suitable than anyone else's.

In addition, the risks of transfusion – such as blood being given to the wrong patient or the recipient experiencing a reaction to the blood – are not eliminated by directed donation.

CHAPTER SEVENTEEN

Treating cancer with chemotherapy and radiotherapy

Many of us find cancer a very frightening disease. Although many cancers now have better survival rates than some common heart and lung conditions, there remains a fear of you, or a loved one, being told you have 'the Big C'. This is not without reason – nearly 30% of all deaths in the UK in 2011 were due to cancer of some sort. However, many cancers can now be treated effectively with surgery, chemotherapy, radiotherapy and other approaches.

Cancer is not one disease, but a very diverse family of diseases in which certain cells in the body start to divide and grow uncontrollably. There are more than 200 different types of cancer that affect the human body, often named after the cell group or type of tissue where they begin. Breast cancer starts in the breast, colon cancer in the bowel and melanoma in the skin. Because cancer cells have stopped behaving normally, they can spread to other parts of the body through the blood and lymphatic systems. Depending on the type of cancer and where it originates, this may be to the lung, the liver, the bone or elsewhere.

While there are many different methods used to treat cancers, three are particularly common. The first is surgery – literally removing the growth. Some tumours are more amenable to this than others. The second is chemotherapy, which is using medicine to kill the cancer cells. The third is radiotherapy, which is the use of radiation (usually X-rays) and radioactive substances to destroy cancer cells. It is not uncommon for people with cancer to receive combinations of these treatments. With thyroid cancer, for example, patients will often have surgery to remove the thyroid gland and then radioactive iodine to kill any remaining cancerous cells.

The aim of this chapter is to give a straightforward introduction to both chemotherapy and radiotherapy. Many people are afraid of these treatments because of the way they have been portrayed in the media and because in the past these treatments were sometimes difficult to endure; modern treatments have many fewer side-effects. Patients who have cancer may also have an operation, and the experience of undergoing surgery for cancer is very similar to any other operation which we have already described in Chapter 15. Organisations like Macmillan Cancer Support and Cancer Research UK have excellent leaflets and comprehensive websites which give information on all aspects of cancer care and support for cancer patients and their families; we encourage anyone affected by cancer to have a look at these (see Appendix).

How are chemotherapy and radiotherapy used to treat cancer?

Both chemotherapy and radiotherapy can be given for a number of different reasons, at different times, and either in isolation or in combination with each other. Treatment may be curative or palliative.

Curative treatment

Curative means, literally, something which cures. Obviously, all doctors who look after people with cancer start with the aim of curing them. Chemotherapy and radiotherapy may be given either separately or in combination to cure certain cancers. Good examples of cancers which are often cured by chemotherapy and/or radiotherapy include Hodgkin's lymphoma and testicular cancer. On other occasions, chemotherapy and radiotherapy need to be used in combination with surgery. One or both can be given before surgery to shrink the tumour, making it safer to remove, or may be given after surgery to kill off any remaining cancer cells and reduce the risk of recurrence (the cancer coming back). The combined treatment beforehand is called 'neo-adjuvant therapy' and afterwards is called 'adjuvant therapy'. An example of using all three approaches is rectal cancer; some patients are cured by having neoadjuvant chemotherapy and radiotherapy together first, followed by surgery, and then finally adjuvant chemotherapy.

Palliative treatment to control symptoms and/or prolong life

Both chemotherapy and radiotherapy can be given even when doctors know that a cure is not possible. This is called 'palliative treatment' and is done for two main reasons. First, it may lengthen the person's life, sometimes significantly. Second, even when death is relatively imminent, it may relieve symptoms such as pain.

Chemotherapy

Chemotherapy drugs disrupt the way cancer cells grow and divide. However, growth and division is also a normal part of the regeneration of many different types of healthy cells in your body. Chemotherapy often affects this process in normal cells as well, causing many of the side-effects associated with it. Chemotherapy can be given on its own, but is often used in combination with other treatments such as surgery, radiotherapy, hormonal therapy or other anti-cancer drugs. Some newer anti-cancer drugs are referred to as 'targeted treatments' or 'biological therapies'. They are directed at specific parts of the cancer cells and work differently to chemotherapy, often using the immune system to help defeat the cancer.

The type of chemotherapy a patient receives depends on the type of cancer, how far it has spread, whether the patient has had chemotherapy before, and a number of other factors. The chemotherapy drugs can be taken in many different ways, depending on the treatment plan specifically designed for each patient. The main methods are as follows:

Oral (by mouth)

Some chemotherapy drugs can be taken as tablets. You will still need to go to hospital for regular check-ups to monitor your treatment and your cancer, but you can take the treatment yourself at home.

Injection (via a needle or cannula)

Various different types of injection can be used. Most people who have chemotherapy by injection have their treatment in an outpatient clinic, although some will need to stay in hospital overnight. Intravenous (IV) chemotherapy is delivered directly into a vein. This can be over a number of hours or days (an infusion) or it can be over a few minutes (a bolus injection). Different methods can be used to access your vein, depending on the drugs you are having and for how long access will be needed to complete the course. It can be painful to have repeated insertions of needles or drips into veins, so longer-term solutions have been developed that allow people to have a special cannula or tube in place for weeks while going about their usual life. Some are 'tunnelled lines' buried under the skin. For some long-term chemotherapy treatments, a chamber can be inserted under the skin and connected to a nearby vein. When chemotherapy is administered, a special needle is placed into the chamber and connected to a drip. The chamber can be kept in place for weeks or months. This is known as a 'portacath', or an implanted or subcutaneous port.

Chemotherapy can also be given by intramuscular or subcutaneous injection, as described in Chapter 15. It can in certain, very special circumstances also be infused into certain spaces in the body to 'wash over' the surfaces. Intrathecal chemotherapy is when chemotherapy is introduced into the space around the brain and spinal cord, and intraperitoneal refers to the infusion of chemotherapy into the abdominal cavity. These are only conducted in specialised units.

Having chemotherapy

Chemotherapy is most often given in a specialist chemotherapy clinic or day unit, run by nurses who are trained in administering these particular medicines. When you arrive in the clinic, you will meet the nurse who will look after you that day. The nurse will do a variety of preliminary checks, including confirming your identity and checking what treatment you are due to receive. You will usually have some blood tests, and you may have to wait for the results to come back from the laboratory to confirm that it is safe for you to have your treatment. Box 19 suggests some questions to ask about your treatment.

Your chemotherapy dose will usually be based on your height and weight, which means that your chemotherapy drugs need to be prepared each time specifically for you. The chemotherapy is prepared by pharmacists, who carry out various checks to make sure the drug and dose is correct before it is made up. Each dose is then double-checked and signed off before it can be delivered to the clinic. You may, therefore, have to wait a while before your dose is ready to be given. Your nurse will then give you the chemotherapy. You may have to wait again in the clinic after receiving the medication, while the nurses monitor you to ensure you do not suffer any adverse reactions to the chemotherapy. Since

> **Box 19** *Questions to ask about your chemotherapy*
>
> - Why am I having chemotherapy?
> - What medicines will I be given?
> - How will I take these medicines?
> - How often will I need to have chemotherapy?
> - How long will I be having chemotherapy treatments for?
> - How long will each treatment last?
> - What side-effects might I have?
> - What side-effects should I report immediately?
> - Are there any long-term effects?
> - How will we know if it's working?
> - What activities should I do or not do to take care of myself?
> - Can I keep working (or going to school) during treatment?
> - Can I have a hospital parking permit or discounted parking rates for my appointments?
> - Can you provide hospital transport for me?
> - Is there somewhere I can stay during my treatment period if it is too far to travel?
> - Where can I get more information about chemotherapy?
> - Who should I contact if I have problems afterwards, and how can I contact them?

you may have to wait for blood results, for your chemotherapy drugs to be made by the pharmacy department or to see your doctor, you might be in the department for a few hours. The clinical team will try to keep the waiting to a minimum, but it may be helpful to take a book, a laptop, or anything you enjoy to help pass the time. You can usually have a relative or friend with you while you are waiting. There may be volunteers who help with drinks or snacks when you need them. Some units also have complementary therapists who provide therapies like reflexology, which can be very helpful for stress and symptom relief.

Side-effects of chemotherapy

Chemotherapy treatment sometimes produces unpleasant side-effects; different drugs and doses cause different side-effects. Some are mild and easily treated; others are more distressing, but can often be reduced or eased with medication. Most side-effects are short-term and usually disappear when chemotherapy is complete. People having high doses of chemotherapy may have more complex side-effects, and are more likely to need to stay in hospital.

Your cancer doctor and nurse specialist should always explain the side-effects that your chemotherapy is likely to cause. Always tell your doctor or nurse about any side-effects you experience. They can usually prescribe medicines to reduce them, or change the medicines you are already taking in the hope of finding a better option for you. Some of the most common side-effects are:

Feeling sick

Some chemotherapy drugs can make you feel sick (nauseated), or actually cause you to be sick (vomit). Not all chemotherapy causes sickness and many people have no sickness at all. If your chemotherapy is known to cause nausea and vomiting, you will be given anti-sickness drugs by injection or as tablets before your chemotherapy. These are very effective treatments and are called 'anti-emetics'. You will also be given tablets to take at home afterwards. You should take these regularly, even if you do not feel sick, unless your doctors suggest otherwise. It is easier to prevent sickness than to treat it once it has started.

Hair loss

Your doctor or specialist nurse will tell you if your type of chemotherapy is likely to cause hair loss. You might notice that your hair does not fall out, but becomes dry and brittle and breaks easily; looking after the condition of your hair can make it less likely to break. Some chemotherapy drugs do cause your hair to fall out, which can be very upsetting. Hair loss usually starts within a few weeks of beginning chemotherapy or, very occasionally, within a few days. Your hair will usually grow back over a few months once you have finished treatment and the hair cells can start dividing and creating new hair again. The new hair will be very fine at first, and may have a slightly different colour or texture than before. You will probably have a full head of hair again after three to six months. The cancer nurses will tell you if you are likely to lose your hair, and explain what support is available to help you through this period.

A sore mouth

Chemotherapy can cause different mouth problems, such as a sore mouth, mouth ulcers or infection. Mouth ulcers can become infected, or you may develop another infection in your mouth. The most common mouth infection is called candidiasis (or 'thrush'). It shows as white spots on your mouth and tongue, or your tongue and mouth lining become red and swollen. Always let your doctor or chemotherapy nurse know if you have mouth ulcers or any other problems with your mouth. They can give you mouthwashes, medicines, lozenges and gels to heal ulcers and to clear or prevent any infection. Thrush is treated with anti-fungal medicines. Dental treatment may need to be delayed during chemotherapy because of the risk of infection and a sore mouth.

Increased risk of infection

Chemotherapy can reduce the number of white bloods cells in your blood, making you susceptible to infection. Your resistance to infection is usually at its lowest 7–14 days after the start of chemotherapy. After that the number of white blood cells will increase steadily, and usually return to normal before your next cycle of chemotherapy is due. You can reduce the chance of infection by taking some simple precautions:

- bathing regularly and washing your hands thoroughly after using the toilet and before preparing food;
- staying away from crowded places and from people who you know have an infection, such as a cold;
- making sure your food is thoroughly cooked and asking your nurse if there are any foods you should avoid.

Watch out for flu-like symptoms and a raised temperature, which may be signs of infection. Your doctor will have told you what to do if this happens. You may need to go to the emergency department or contact your specialist nurse. If you are at a high risk of infection, you may receive injections to boost your immune system.

Radiotherapy

Radiotherapy is the use of radiation, usually X-rays, to treat illness. About 40% of people with cancer have radiotherapy as part of their treatment. Radiotherapy works by destroying the cancer cells in the treated area. Although normal cells are also affected by the radiation, they are better at repairing themselves than the cancer cells.

Radiotherapy can be given in two main ways:

- from outside the body, as 'external radiotherapy', using either X-rays from machines called linear accelerators or other types of radiation;
- from within the body, as 'internal radiotherapy', by drinking or having a liquid injected that is taken up by cancer cells, or by putting radioactive material in or close to a tumour.

The radiotherapy team plan each patient's radiotherapy individually. Their aim is to give the highest possible dose to the cancer, but as low a dose as possible to the surrounding healthy cells.

In this way they hope the cancer will be destroyed, or at least significantly shrunk, while the side-effects are minimised and the healthy cells can recover afterwards.

Having external radiotherapy

External radiotherapy is normally given as a series of short, daily outpatient treatments in the radiotherapy department, using equipment similar to a large X-ray machine. Radiotherapy machines vary slightly in how they look and how they work. The most common type of machine is called a linear accelerator machine (LINAC), which uses electricity to create the radiotherapy beams.

Curative radiotherapy (to destroy a tumour) usually involves having a course of treatment once a day for a number of weeks, often with a break at the weekends. Some people may have more than one treatment each day, or a treatment every day including weekends. Giving the treatment in small doses over time means that less damage is done to normal cells than to cancer cells, which reduces the side-effects of radiotherapy. Palliative radiotherapy (to control symptoms) can be very effective, and can involve anything from one to ten sessions of treatment depending on the disease. Box 20 suggests questions to ask about your radiotherapy treatment.

The staff who give the radiotherapy treatment are called radiographers. They will explain the whole process to you, which will become familiar after a couple of sessions. A radiotherapy session takes between 10 and 30 minutes. The first time you visit will involve a planning session, when the radiographer will discuss your treatment with you and make two or three permanent pinpoint tattoo marks on your skin. The radiographer uses these to line up the radiotherapy machine for each treatment. This makes sure that you have exactly the same area treated each time. These marks are very small, little more than a pin head or freckle.

Box 20 *Questions to ask about your radiotherapy*

- Why are you prescribing radiotherapy for me?
- What kind of radiotherapy treatment will I have?
- Will it be my only treatment or will I have other treatments too?
- Are you trying to cure me, help me live longer or reduce my symptoms? Or a combination of these?
- What is your plan for my treatment?
- How many sessions of treatment will I have?
- How long will the treatment last?
- Where will I have my treatment?
- Can I have the same treatment again in the future if I need to?
- What are the likely side-effects of this treatment?
- Can I have a hospital parking permit or discounted parking rates for my appointments?
- Can you provide hospital transport for me?
- Is there somewhere I can stay during my treatment period if it is too far to travel?
- Where can I get more information about radiotherapy?

The delivery of the radiation dose itself only lasts a few minutes; most of the appointment is spent getting you into position and doing various checks. Before your treatment you may be asked to take off some of your clothes (from the area of your body that needs treating) and to put on a hospital gown. This is so that the radiographers can easily access the marks on your skin that show the treatment area. When the radiographers are ready for you, they will position you carefully on the treatment couch and adjust its height and position. It is important that you are comfortable, as you have to lie as still as possible during the treatment.

Once you are in the correct position, the radiographers will leave the room. This is because a small amount of radiation scatters through the room. This does not affect you, but could affect the staff over time; they are there every day and the cumulative effect of radiation could be harmful to them. During the treatment the radiographers will watch you from the next room through a window or via a camera. Many treatment rooms also have an intercom so the radiographers can talk to you while you have your treatment. If you have any problems, you can speak to them through the intercom and they will come in to help you. If there is no intercom in the room, the radiographers will let you know how you can attract their attention. They will also take care to protect your privacy so that nobody else can see you.

The treatment itself is painless. You may hear a slight buzzing noise from the radiotherapy machine while your treatment is being given. The machine does not normally touch you, although for some types of skin cancer it may press against your skin.

Most curative radiotherapy involves having treatment from several different directions. This means that during your treatment the radiotherapy machine will automatically stop and move into a new position before your treatment continues. This may happen several times and you will need to stay still. Occasionally, the radiographers will come into the treatment room to change the position of the machine. Once your treatment session has finished, the radiographers will return and will help you off the treatment couch. You will then be able to get ready to go home or back to the ward.

Having internal radiotherapy

There are two main types of internal radiotherapy:
- *Brachytherapy*. A solid radioactive source is placed into or close to the tumour.
- *Radioisotope treatment*. A liquid source of radiation is used inside the body. This is also called radionuclide therapy.

Brachytherapy gives a high dose of radiotherapy directly to the tumour, but only a low dose to normal tissues. It is mainly used to treat cancers in the prostate gland, cervix and womb, but can also be used to treat some other cancers, such as head and neck cancers. For instance, small radioactive seeds can be inserted into a prostate tumour and left to release their radioactivity slowly. The seeds are not removed and the radiation gradually fades away over about six months.

The brachytherapy process varies according to the type of cancer. Typically you will visit the hospital for a planning session in which staff plot the precise location of the cancer and work out how much of the radioactive material to use in the treatment. You will then have a second session to insert the radioactive material, which might take up to an hour. You will have an anaesthetic so that you do not feel any pain during the procedure. This may be a general anaesthetic (so that you are asleep) or a regional or local anaesthetic (so that you are awake but not able to feel anything in the area concerned). (See Chapter 15 for more information on anaesthesia.) Sometimes both the planning session and the treatment take place on the same day. Depending on what time of day you have your treatment, you may need to stay in hospital for one night or you may be able to go home the same day.

Radioisotopes (the second type of internal radiotherapy) are types of medication with radioactive properties that are given by mouth as a drink or capsules, or are injected into a vein. Cancer cells absorb the radioisotope more than the normal cells do, and receive a higher dose of radioactivity. This causes the cancer cells to die. Before you have any treatment with a radioisotope, you will be given more detailed information about it.

Side-effects of radiotherapy

Radiotherapy destroys cancer cells in the targeted area of the body. However, the treatment can also affect some of the normal cells nearby. Radiotherapy affects people in different ways, so it is difficult to predict exactly how a particular person will react. Some people have only mild side-effects; for others the side-effects are more severe.

External radiotherapy tends to cause more side-effects than internal therapy. Most people will have only a few of the side-effects mentioned here, and severe side-effects are rare with modern radiotherapy; for many people they will be mild. Most will continue for about 10–15 days after treatment has finished and then gradually disappear. The main side-effects are described below:

Tiredness

Many people feel tired during their period of radiotherapy treatment. The tiredness can continue for weeks to months after your treatment has finished. Try to get plenty of rest, but balance this with some gentle exercise, such as short walks. This will give you more energy and help to keep your muscles working. Some people are able to continue working, but many need to take time off work.

Feeling sick

Some people find that their treatment makes them feel sick, and they may actually vomit. This is more likely to happen if the treatment area is near the stomach or small bowel. Be sure to tell your doctor or radiographer if you feel sick, as medication can be prescribed to reduce these effects. If you are given anti-sickness tablets, take them regularly as this is the best way to keep the nausea controlled.

Skin reactions

Some people develop a skin reaction while having external radiotherapy. If you develop a skin reaction, such as soreness or a change in skin colour, you should tell the radiotherapy staff as soon as possible. They will advise you on the best way to manage it.

Flu-like symptoms

You may experience flu-like symptoms, including headaches, aching joints or muscles and lack of energy. They do not usually last long. Drinking plenty of fluids and getting plenty of rest can help.

Hair loss

Radiotherapy may cause hair loss, usually starting about two to three weeks after the treatment begins. Hair should grow back after treatment finishes, although this may take several months and will depend on the dose of radiotherapy you have had.

Longer-term effects

Most side-effects are short-lived and modern radiotherapy increasingly limits the risk of long-term side-effects. However, when radiotherapy is given with chemotherapy, the long-term effects of radiotherapy may be increased. Before you agree to either chemotherapy or radiotherapy, your doctor will discuss the likelihood of you developing long-term side-effects. It is important that you have the opportunity to talk through these possibilities even though they might not happen to you.

Being supported during cancer treatment

Apart from the doctors and nurses that you see on the ward, there are several other healthcare professionals who can answer your questions or provide extra help. Clinical nurse specialists will be able to answer most of your queries about the treatment process, and hospital pharmacists will be able to give detailed information about your chemotherapy and other medication. All hospitals treating cancer will have specialist pain teams to deal with pain that is not responding to ordinary painkillers. Macmillan Cancer nurses may be able to provide support in hospital and at home. Some hospitals have a 'Maggie's Centre' for cancer patients and their families, where you can ask for help or advice, or simply relax and unwind in a comfortable and friendly environment. Many cancer units have support groups led by patients who have previously had the disease or undergone similar treatments and their families and friends. Talking to people who have had similar experiences in their lives and truly understand what you are going through is enormously helpful for most people.

Staying well
in hospital

CHAPTER EIGHTEEN

Looking after yourself

We have used many pages of this book explaining what happens in hospital and what people will do when investigating and treating your condition. It may seem that there is nothing much that you can do except wait to go home. However, there is actually a lot you can do to make your stay in hospital more pleasant and more comfortable. Naturally there may be times, such as when you are recovering from an operation or when you are very ill, when all you can manage to do is sleep or lie in bed. Even then, though, there are active steps you can take to ensure you remain empowered and involved in your care. Once you feel better, it does help your recovery if you get up and move around (as long as you are allowed to do so by your clinical team), talk to friends and family, and carry on with your usual activities and interests. In this chapter we offer some suggestions about making your hospital stay easier and more comfortable.

What to take with you

The hospital will provide for all your medical care, but will not provide day-to-day clothes or personal toiletries except in emergencies. You need to plan for a stay in what is essentially a rather basic and noisy hotel – one that may not score very well on a travel review website! You will probably have a small cupboard by your bed in which to keep your personal belongings. In some wards you may not be allowed to keep anything on top of the cupboard, to make it easier to clean the surfaces. However,

Box 21 *Things to consider taking to hospital*

- Your appointment card or admission letter
- Two nightdresses or pairs of pyjamas (depending on the length of your stay)
- Day clothes for when you feel stronger and want to get up. Hospital wards are often kept very warm, so bear this in mind when choosing clothes.
- Clean underwear
- A dressing gown and slippers
- A small hand towel
- Toiletries, including soap, a toothbrush, toothpaste, shampoo and conditioner, and a bag to put them in
- Sanitary towels or tampons
- A razor and shaving materials
- A comb or hairbrush
- Ear plugs, a mask to cover your eyes and anything else that helps you sleep
- Things to occupy you, such as books, magazines or puzzle books
- Photographs and reminders of home and family
- A small amount of money to buy newspapers, make phone calls and buy anything you may want from the hospital shop or ward trolley
- A list of your usual medicines, and supplies of medicines that you usually take, including nicotine replacement treatment, eye drops, inhalers and creams
- A notebook and pen to write down any questions you have when the doctor is not available
- Your address book and important phone numbers, including your GP's name, address and telephone number
- Any particular home comforts that might help you feel at home – your own pillow, perhaps, or a familiar and comfortable item of clothing?
- Snacks to eat if you are hungry between meals

you should have enough space for a few items of clothing, magazines, toiletries and personal items such as photographs. You should consider bringing a notebook to record any questions you might have for the staff looking after you, or to keep a record of what has happened – who you saw, what medicines you were given, and any other useful information. Box 21 gives some suggestions as to what you may want to bring in yourself or ask others to bring in for you.

Hospitals are very busy places, with many staff and visitors. It is easy for things to get lost and there is also the possibility that something might be stolen. (Sadly, thieves can sometimes target hospitals, although this is rare.) Some wards have a safe in which you can leave valuable items if you are concerned about security, but it is best to avoid bringing jewellery, credit cards or other precious items into hospital. If you do give anything to the hospital for safekeeping, you should be given a receipt.

Preparing in advance for your return home

When thinking about what to take to hospital, you should also think about returning home afterwards. You are likely to be tired after your discharge from hospital, and may not be able to move around as easily. You may be in some discomfort, so make sure you have some basic painkillers at home. If you live on your own, we suggest that you consider putting some bread and milk in the freezer, and make sure you have enough food to last until you or a friend or family member can go shopping. You may also want to arrange for someone to check your home while you are away. If your admission to hospital was not planned in advance, you may want to telephone a friend or neighbour and ask them to check on your home and to buy some basic groceries for you on your return.

Depending on the treatment you receive, your mobility might be restricted when you are returning home from hospital. Put your TV remote control, books and magazines, radio, telephone, tissues, and anything else you may need on a table next to where you are likely to spend most of your time. There is nothing more frustrating than being unable to get the things you need because you are immobile!

Mobile phones and electrical equipment

The NHS recognises the importance of patients keeping in touch with family and friends. Each hospital will have a policy on the use of mobile phones and the hospital should display signs showing where you can and cannot use a mobile phone. You will usually be able to make calls and send texts in the hospital entrance or reception, in communal areas such as cafes and lift lobbies, in day rooms on wards, and in other areas where no investigations or treatments are carried out. If you need to make a call or send a text message, make sure you go to an area where you can use your phone. If you are not sure, ask a member of staff.

You should not use your phone to take photographs, because all patients and visitors are entitled to privacy while in hospital. Some maternity units may permit photos to be taken with a mobile phone – for example, of parents with their newborn baby – as long as no staff, other patients or visitors, or other babies, are in the photo.

Mobile phones and other electronic equipment are still banned in some areas. This is because interference from mobile phones could theoretically stop medical equipment from working properly. Dialysis machines, defibrillators, ventilators, monitors and pumps could all be affected. Loud ring tones and alarms on mobile phones can also be confused with alarms on medical equipment, and if everyone uses their mobile phones all the time, the noise can be very disruptive for patients and staff. Please do not use your telephone in any area unless you are sure it is allowed, for the safety of yourself and others.

Eating and drinking

Having enough to eat and drink when you are in hospital is an important part of your recovery. You should have access to fresh drinking water at all times, unless you need to limit your fluid intake for clinical reasons. Drinking small amounts often will keep you well hydrated. Do ask a member of staff if you need your water jug filling up. Despite numerous campaigns to improve hospital food, it is still, regrettably, very variable in quality. Many hospitals no longer prepare food on the premises. Instead, the food is brought in and reheated. Typically the hospital has a contract with a large company which provides the food along with other services. They may not be specialist caterers, and sometimes it shows! Staff can also find it difficult to get decent food, particularly at night.

Malnutrition is a major problem in hospitals for a number of reasons. First, energy requirements go up considerably when a person is ill, as the body needs energy to heal. Second, many diseases interfere with the body's ability to consume, digest and metabolise food. Third, people's appetite and their access to good, palatable food are both often reduced. Finally, in some hospitals patients can become even more malnourished because, unfortunately, staff do not appreciate the difficulties they have with feeding themselves. The charity Age UK issued a report called 'Hungry to be heard', showing that most hospitals give patients all the help they need but some still do not do enough. Staff should be aware that helping patients to eat and drink is an essential part of nursing care. If you are concerned about this for yourself or a family member, do raise it with a senior nurse (see Box 22).

Most hospital wards now operate a 'protected meal times' system. This means that only clinical and catering staff are allowed on the wards during meal times. Visitors may be asked

> **Box 22** *Help with eating and ordering*
>
> Let staff know if you:
> - need help filling in your menu card;
> - find menu choices unsuitable due to allergies, or cultural or personal preferences;
> - find it hard to reach your meal or drink;
> - have difficulty cutting your food or opening cartons;
> - prefer smaller meals with between-meal snacks;
> - have trouble chewing or swallowing.

to leave or may be prevented from entering a ward, and all other ward activities such as ward rounds, blood tests and medication rounds cease. This ensures that nursing staff are available to assist patients where necessary, and that patients can eat their food without distraction.

You will probably be asked to complete a menu card each day to say what you would like to eat. Sometimes these are distributed a day ahead, so you are choosing your food for the following day. It can be hard to predict what you will want to eat for dinner tomorrow and there may be alternative arrangements for food on your ward. Some wards have facilities that provide snacks or lighter meals. We advocate having access to your own snacks and food by having some brought in from home or buying some from the hospital shop or trolley. In the vast majority of cases, the clinicians looking after you will be happy for you to eat and drink anything you like if it keeps your energy intake up. However, some wards have strict rules about the types of food that can be brought in. Foods such as meat or fish, cream-based products, eggs or take-away items may be restricted or banned altogether, because they can go off and cause infections which can spread very easily. Normally, bottled or canned drinks and dry foods such as biscuits, nuts, dried fruit, chocolates and crisps are allowed. Check with your ward staff about the local policy.

Hospitals should cater for your personal dietary needs. Let staff know if you need a particular type of food such as kosher, gluten-free, halal, vegetarian or vegan. Speak to a senior nurse as soon as possible if you have special requirements, problems reading the menu or concerns about your diet. If you feel you have lost weight, lost your appetite, or need help, advice or support relating to what you are eating, you can be referred to a dietician.

Alcohol and tobacco

You will not be allowed to bring alcohol into hospital and you will not be allowed to smoke inside the hospital. Most hospitals ban smoking anywhere within the hospital grounds, including outside. Being in hospital is a fantastic opportunity to give up smoking and staff will be able to help you. Your doctor can prescribe nicotine replacement therapy to help you do this.

Sleeping and resting

We all know the importance of a good night's sleep. When we are ill or in pain, we are even more in need of sleep. However, hospitals are often rather noisy places as investigations and treatments go on 24 hours a day. Patients who are seriously ill, especially those in intensive care, are monitored continually and may need to be woken during the night and at other times when they are sleeping. You may also hear the beeping of monitors and alarms, either attached to you or to a patient nearby.

Staff on the wards will do their best to create an atmosphere for sleep by minimising the amount of activity and turning down the lights, but inevitably there will be some disturbance at times. What can you do to help yourself? There are many tips for getting a good night's sleep and you will know those that suit you, whether they involve a hot drink or counting sheep! Use whatever techniques help you generally. However, there are a few issues that are particularly relevant in hospitals:

Make it dark at night. A dark room will encourage your body to go into a deep sleep. The monitors and other lights in a typical hospital room may give off too much light for you to rest easily. Find a good sleep mask to wear when you want to sleep.

Mask noise. Hospital rooms can be noisy, especially if you have another patient beside you. Get a music player and download some favourite calming music, podcasts, or even white noise (a type of noise that sounds like static and muffles other noise) – or purchase a soft pair of earplugs. Use them as needed, especially if you would like to take a nap during the day when the wards are busy.

Get some light during the day. During the day, especially around midday, try to get some exposure to light. If you can walk or use a wheelchair, go outside or at least to the window. Ask that the curtains be opened. Getting daylight exposure will help your body know what time of day it is, which will allow you to sleep better at night. This may be particularly important in help-ing elderly patients keep orientated in what can often be a quite disorientating environment.

Talk to the staff. Tell your nurses and doctors that you really want to make sleep a priority. Ask them to disturb you as few times as possible during the night. They will do what they can to help you get your sleep. They may prescribe a sleeping tablet for night-time if all other efforts fail; this can be a useful back-up, so ask if one has been prescribed.

Find the right temperature. Being at the right temperature is also important for a good night's sleep. Hospital wards are generally very warm, so wearing light nightclothes may help. Speak to the nursing staff if you are still too hot; it may be possible to have a fan in your room.

Getting out and taking exercise

You may assume that being in hospital means being in bed. In days gone by, hospital patients did indeed spend much of their time in bed as this was thought to help recovery. However, we now know that staying in bed for too long can increase the chances of a variety of health problems, such as muscle weakness, infections, pressure ulcers and blood clots (see Chapter 20). When you are feeling very ill, you should of course spend more time in bed. You need to be looked after and the staff are there to take care of you. However, as you begin to recover, you will be encouraged to get up. Even after a major operation you may be asked to start walking the very next day. This may seem rather daunting, but becoming active as soon as you are able to will help your recovery by improving muscle tone and opening the lungs up to breathe more easily. Obviously, if you are feeling weak you must make sure you wait for a member of staff to support you; this may be the ward physiotherapist. Being active will probably also improve your mental well-being. Getting off the ward if possible to get some fresh air, buy a newspaper or get something to eat or drink tends to cheer people up.

Fighting helplessness

When you are ill, it is very difficult not to feel anxious, nervous, tired and sometimes helpless. This is normal and understandable. However, we encourage you to try and fight this feeling as much as you can. One of the problems with being in hospital, as we have mentioned before, is that people can easily become passive or defeatist. Regularly, when on the wards and talking to patients, we see people who are able to dress themselves independently choosing to wear pyjamas in the middle of the day. We see patients who are waiting to ask permission to go to the bathroom or use the shower, or who stop being responsible for their own self-care. Sometimes this cannot be helped, of course, and we are not advocating recklessness; if you are unable to do certain things, ask for help. But we really encourage you to stay as independent as possible, both in body and in mind, throughout your time in hospital, and to treat the days as you would in your own home. You should remain your normal independent-minded self, unless limited by illness.

CHAPTER NINETEEN

Preventing infection

Infections are caused by micro-organisms such as bacteria, viruses, parasites or fungi, and can be spread – directly or indirectly – from one person to another. There is always a risk that you can acquire a new infection while in hospital. Most medical organisations invest a lot of time and effort in trying to prevent healthcare-associated infections because the consequences to patients can be so serious. The good news is that patients, staff and visitors can all help reduce the spread of these infections with a few simple precautions, the most important of which is to make sure hands are kept clean at all times.

What are healthcare-associated infections?

We are often exposed to infection in daily life and most of these infections do not usually cause any major problems in healthy individuals. However, infections can be much more dangerous for people who are already unwell or who are having an operation. Certain groups of people, such as young children, the elderly and people with reduced immunity, are particularly at risk of becoming very unwell if they get an infection, sometimes with life-threatening consequences.

Healthcare-associated infections are infections picked up by people who come into contact with the healthcare system. One of the reasons the micro-organisms (sometimes referred to as 'germs' or 'bugs') that cause these infections are more common in places such as hospitals is because of the greater need to use antibiotics. The use of antibiotics sometimes allows resistance to develop, which then makes the micro-organisms harder to treat.

Antibiotics can also kill some 'good bacteria' in our bodies, which normally keep the 'bad bacteria' in check; the use of antibiotics can upset that balance. Another reason is the number of people moving around and coming into contact with each other. Healthcare workers and hospital visitors can pick up troublesome germs from patients or contaminated surfaces and, if they are not careful, transmit the germs to other patients without even realising.

You may already have heard of some of the more widely-publicised healthcare-associated infections, such as MRSA (which stands for methicillin-resistant *Staphylococcus aureus*, the name of the bacterium that causes the infection), but there are also many others. Such bacteria can cause infections in different parts of the body, including the skin, bone, lungs, urinary system and bowels. They can also cause infection of surgical wounds, and may enter the body via medical equipment such as artificial lung ventilators, joint replacements and urinary catheters. There is no need to know about all the different types of infection, but it is helpful to understand why healthcare-associated infections are taken so seriously and what you can do to help prevent them.

Clean hands are the key to infection control

Good hand hygiene is probably the most effective way to prevent the spread of infection. Germs are very easily passed from one person to another by direct physical contact with other people, especially by doctors, nurses and other healthcare professionals who interact with large numbers of patients on a daily basis. Most hospitals have been able to significantly reduce the rates of healthcare-associated infection in recent years by ensuring that staff always clean their hands at the 'five moments' recommended by the World Health Organization (see Box 23). Healthcare professionals may be very busy, and may occasionally forget to clean their hands before touching you or another patient. If you think that a member of staff has forgotten to clean their hands, you should always feel free to politely remind them to do so before coming into contact with you or your relative.

> **Box 23** *The World Health Organization's 'five moments' of hand hygiene*
>
> - Before patient contact (such as shaking hands, helping a patient to move around, clinical examination)
> - Before aseptic tasks (such as wound dressing, catheter insertion, preparing food or medication)
> - After body fluid exposure risk (such as taking a blood sample, dental care, clearing up urine or faeces)
> - After patient contact (such as shaking hands, helping a patient to move around, clinical examination)
> - After contact with patient surroundings (such as changing bed linen, adjusting equipment)

Effective hand hygiene is achieved by applying alcohol-based hand gels and by washing hands thoroughly with soap and water. Using gel is quick and convenient, but regular handwashing with soap and water is also necessary, particularly with one type of bacteria – *Clostridium difficile* – which causes diarrhoea and abdominal pain and is not killed by alcohol gel.

Using alcohol hand gels

Alcohol hand gels are widely available in all UK hospitals as part of a national drive to reduce healthcare-associated infection. They are usually placed at the entrance to the hospital, at the entrance to wards, near each bedside and in other locations. Ask the staff where the nearest dispenser is if you cannot see it.

To clean your hands effectively, it is important that the gel is applied all over the hands and fingers. You will need a small pool of gel in a cupped hand. There should be diagrams near to the dispensers in the hospital showing how to apply it to cover all surfaces of the hands, to make sure that any germs living on the skin of the hands are killed. It is important to follow these instructions. The gel dries within 20–30 seconds, and can be used as often as you like. Frequent use of the gel can cause hands to become a bit dry, so some hospitals keep a moisturising cream in dispensers nearby to help counteract this.

When you should wash with soap and water

Alcohol hand gels can be used when there is no obvious contamination of the hands (on hands that look clean to the naked eye) and when there has been no known contact with bodily fluids (such as saliva or urine). They are quick, convenient and effective. However, there are some situations where washing hands with soap and water is needed as well.

When hands are visibly dirty, or after possible contact with any bodily fluids or people with diarrhoea, you should wash with soap and water because alcohol gel can be ineffective in this situation. As with using alcohol hand gels, there is a specific way to wash your hands effectively and there should be diagrams near to handwashing sinks in the hospital. If you follow this guide, you will make sure that all parts of your hands are clean, even the parts that are difficult to clean or frequently forgotten. You should always wash your hands with soap and water before eating as part of good hygiene, of course, rather than just use the gel. This has the added benefit of washing off any gel, which – if it gets onto food – actually has a very bitter taste.

Other ways of preventing hospital-associated infections

Some other infection control measures may be put in place to protect certain patients. Patients with contagious conditions such as infectious diarrhoea are often asked to move into side-rooms to reduce the risk of the infection spreading to other patients.

In such cases, staff and visitors may be asked to wear disposable plastic gloves and aprons to stop their skin and clothes from picking up the germs that cause diarrhoea. In some parts of the hospital, such as intensive care units and wards caring for patients with low resistance to infection, staff and visitors may be asked to wear gloves and aprons at all times to reduce the risk of spreading infection; these gloves and aprons are changed in between seeing different patients. There will be a sign indicating if infection control precautions such as these are in place, and ward staff will be able to show visitors what they need to do. If you are not sure, do ask the ward staff. You may feel silly wearing gloves and an apron, but these precautions protect both you and your relative or friend.

A small proportion of the healthy general public carry bacteria that can cause hospital-associated infections without realising it, and this is particularly true for MRSA. These people are referred to as 'carriers' and have no symptoms of infection. The MRSA or other bacterium just lives on the surface of their body. Many hospitals routinely screen patients for MRSA before they come in for planned treatments such as surgery. If a patient is found to be carrying MRSA, they may be asked to take some additional precautions before they come into hospital. This may include bathing with special antibacterial soaps, or using powders and creams to eradicate the germs. This is because MRSA may be harmless before the patient has an operation, but can become dangerous afterwards when the process of surgery reduces the patient's resistance to infection.

Protecting yourself and your family

The most important thing you can do is to be vigilant when you are in the hospital. You should practise good hand hygiene and remind others to do the same, including visitors, other patients and staff. You can also keep an eye out for the general cleanliness of surfaces, floors and equipment. If you do see something that is dirty, do not touch it or clean it yourself, but inform a member of staff so that they can safely decontaminate the area. Finally, remember that you must always protect yourself by washing your hands before eating, after using the toilet, or if you are sick or are splashed or touched by any other bodily fluids.

CHAPTER TWENTY

Preventing deep vein thrombosis

A deep vein thrombosis (DVT) is an abnormal blood clot ('thrombosis') that develops in the deep veins of the body, such as those found in the pelvis and legs. For a number of reasons, people in hospital are at increased risk of a DVT. This chapter explains what causes a DVT, how it is prevented and what you can do to reduce the risks.

What is a deep vein thrombosis?

Blood is normally a liquid within the body but in certain circumstances, such as when there is bleeding after a cut, blood becomes solid; this is known as 'clotting'. The formation of a blood clot is useful when you cut yourself, because it stops the bleeding from continuing. However, occasionally clots can also form inside the veins, particularly in the legs, which reduces or stops the flow of blood in that part of the body. These are DVTs, which will usually cause pain and swelling in the affected area. These clots can also move around the body in the blood stream and cause blockages in the blood vessels that supply the lungs. The resulting blockage is a serious condition called 'pulmonary embolism'; it can lead to breathlessness, chest pain and the coughing up of blood, and can sadly on certain occasions be fatal. You may hear the term venous thromboembolism (or VTE) used, which includes both DVT and pulmonary embolism.

Many types of illness or injury, particularly those requiring admission to hospital, increase the risk of DVT (see Box 24). For

---

Box 24 *Factors that increase the risk of deep vein thrombosis*

- Older age
- Smoking
- Being significantly overweight
- Having certain types of operation, such as orthopaedic, pelvic or complex surgery
- Being much less active than usual – for example, after an operation
- Being dehydrated
- Cancer and other inflammatory conditions
- Pregnancy or recent delivery of a baby
- Some medicines – including some forms of hormone replacement therapy and oral contraceptives, although the impact these have on your risk is small
- Specific blood conditions such as thrombophilia that make clots more likely to form
- Previous DVT (either yourself or a close relative)

---

this reason, many people admitted to hospital will receive some form of treatment to prevent DVT even if they are only staying for a short time.

Reducing the risk of DVT before coming into hospital

If you are overweight or a smoker, you can reduce the risk of a DVT in hospital by trying to lose weight and stop smoking before you are admitted; your GP or local pharmacist can offer advice and support. Women who are having an operation and taking an oestrogen-containing oral contraceptive (the 'combined pill') or hormone replacement therapy may be advised to stop taking these drugs four weeks before their operation takes place. If you decide to stop taking the pill, your healthcare team should advise you about other forms of contraception.

Reducing the risk of DVT in hospital

On admission to hospital, every patient should be assessed for their risk of DVT. A member of staff, usually a junior doctor, will assess your risk of having a DVT together with your risk of bleeding. If the risk of a DVT is higher than the risk of bleeding, then some form of DVT prevention will be recommended. You may be given a leaflet that discusses this and other options for reducing the risk during and after your stay. Every patient should then be assessed again within 24 hours of admission and whenever their condition changes significantly. Most people will have some

---

Box 25 *Reducing your risk of deep vein thrombosis while in hospital*

- Keep wearing your compression stockings if you have been advised to wear them. (They can be uncomfortable, but not as uncomfortable as a DVT!)
- Follow any advice you are given to keep moving in bed, which may include hourly exercises such as wiggling your toes and bending your ankles and legs.
- Get up and move around as much as possible.
- Stay well-hydrated by drinking water if possible. As a general guide, two to three litres of water a day is about the right amount unless you are told otherwise by your medical team.
- If you have not been given compression stockings or pre-scribed an anticoagulant drug, ask why not and whether you might need them.
- If you notice that you have swelling or pain in your legs (particularly if only on one side), let a member of staff know immediately.

form of anti-DVT treatment, as everyone has a slightly higher risk simply by being in hospital. This usually includes wearing special anti-DVT compression stockings and receiving antico-agulant drugs to reduce the ability of the blood to clot. If you are not given compression stockings or anticoagulant drugs, ask the nursing staff or doctors if there is a specific reason for this. For instance, you might not be given these if you already have poor blood supply in your leg or foot or have an injury in this area. There are also some important things you can do yourself to reduce your risk of DVT (see Box 25).

Compression stockings (TEDS – thromboembolic deterrent stockings)

These tight elastic stockings, also known as anti-embolism stock-ings, squeeze the blood vessels in the legs, help blood circula-tion, and therefore stop the blood from staying too long in the veins where they might form a clot. The stockings can be a little uncomfortable, but are important for reducing the risk of a DVT. They should be taken off at least once a day to clean and check the skin underneath, usually when showering or bathing, before they are put straight back on. As they are quite tight-fitting, they can be a bit difficult to put on – ask a member of staff if you need help or if you are not sure if you have put them on correctly. It is important that they fit properly. You may be asked to continue wearing anti-embolism stockings after you go home, until you have returned to your normal level of activity.

Anticoagulant drugs

The other main method of DVT prevention is the use of drugs to help prevent blood clots from forming. These are often used as well as compression stockings. The most commonly used drugs are various types of heparin, usually given every day as an injection just under the skin of the abdomen or thigh.

People usually describe the experience of having this injection as a short-lived stinging sensation. There may be some bruising around the injection site, and occasionally a small swelling which will go away after a week or two. After some operations you may also be advised to keep using the anticoagulant medication for a few weeks after you go home, particularly if you have had a cancer operation (see the patient story below). If you need to use it at home, a member of staff will show you, or a member of your family, how to inject the drug just under your skin. The most common reasons why you may not be given an anticoagulant are if you are currently bleeding or have recently had a stroke. You should always ask about both the benefits and the risks of this medication to be sure it is right for you.

....

❝❝ *After my operation, the consultant had settled on ten days of heparin injections. I was lucky – some people have it for longer. Keen to get out of hospital and back to my own bed, I didn't pay much attention to the instructions I'd been given in hospital. And when the nurses gave me the injection on the ward I wasn't paying too much attention either. So when I got home with my injections, I wasn't very keen on having to give them myself, but I knew the importance of having them and decided I had to do it.*

The instructions said to put the injection in your tummy. Mine was very sore, with a big wound across the middle. I decided I didn't want to go near the sore bits, so settled on my leg. I took the injection out and decided I wasn't feeling brave enough to do it myself, so asked my sister to do it for me. She said no, she couldn't inflict pain on me, so I decided I had to be brave and do it myself. I tried to remember the important points – rotate injection sites, inject at the same time each day, take care in pulling off the needle cap and don't touch the needle, hold the fat fold (as I called it) to ensure the injection entered the fatty tissue, don't rub the site afterwards, dispose in the sharps bin. So much to remember!

But I did it. Stabbed myself in the leg, trying to press the plunger without pulling out the needle at the same time. It stung for a moment, but I managed OK. The second night I pulled out the needle too soon, and realised I'd probably lost 50% of the injection. The third night I had a small bump where I'd injected the night before, and the fourth night I got a bruise. Finally, by the sixth night I managed to give it with no problems, completed the course and didn't get a DVT.

In hindsight, my lesson learnt would be to try and practise before going home, ideally observing an injection being given by the nurse one day and then injecting yourself under supervision the next day. 🙷

What happens if I develop a DVT?

If your leg or another area of the body becomes swollen or tender, or there are changes in the skin colour or temperature, you should tell the staff immediately as this could be a DVT. Nurses and doctors should in any case be watching for such signs in their routine assessments of all patients. If your doctor suspects that you might have a DVT, they will first ask for a scan of your leg, usually a specialised ultrasound scan. Lubricant jelly is placed on the leg, and a small, hand-held piece of equipment connected to a computer screen is moved up and down the surface of the leg to check for clots in the veins. If a blood clot is confirmed, treatment is given in the form of anticoagulant medicine; this prevents the clot getting any bigger, gives the body a chance to break down the clot, and prevents it recurring. In the first few weeks this medicine will probably be in the form of heparin injections; these are the same or similar to the drugs used to prevent DVTs, but at a higher dose. As time goes on, these daily injections may be replaced by anticoagulant tablets. The duration of treatment will be tailored to your individual circumstances, but most patients receive anticoagulant treatment for at least three months after suffering a DVT.

CHAPTER TWENTY-ONE

Getting more help

Many admissions to hospital to undergo routine tests, operations and treatments run a fairly predictable course. They may not be familiar to you as a patient, but the staff will know what will typically happen from day to day, how much discomfort you are likely to feel and how long you are likely to be in hospital.

However, sometimes things are not as straightforward as anticipated. Your illness may turn out to be more serious than you had hoped, the treatment may not go completely according to plan, or you may have an illness which is much less predictable. Particularly if you are seriously ill, you may also be as worried about your loved ones as you are about yourself. For one reason or another, there are times when each of us needs more help – when we are in pain, when we are distressed, when we seem to be getting sicker, or when we feel lonely, isolated or afraid. In this chapter we discuss what to do if you are in pain, if your condition is deteriorating, if you are feeling very stressed or if there are problems with your treatment. The main message of this chapter, as in the rest of this book, is that you should always make your needs known and ask for help if necessary.

If you are in pain

A stay in hospital may involve some pain and discomfort, but this should generally be short-lived. Receiving an injection or having blood samples taken is not pleasant, but a skilful nurse, doctor or phlebotomist can manage the process quickly and is often able to distract you while they are doing it. After an operation or during a serious illness you may suffer discomfort or pain. In days gone by there were few effective pain-relieving drugs. More recently, although better drugs had been developed, pain was often poorly managed in hospital. Today pain is regarded as an essential 'vital sign', to be regularly checked and recorded in the same way as your temperature, blood pressure and heart rate. Staff have a professional responsibility to check your pain levels and treat any pain as effectively as they can. This should be a continuous process throughout your hospital stay.

Speaking up when you are in pain

People experience pain in different ways, and have different thresholds and attitudes to enduring it. All of us are likely to feel anxious, scared or low in hospital at times and this can increase our sensitivity to pain. Some people find pain of any kind worrying and hard to bear. Others, with different pain thresholds, are much less troubled by aches and pains. However, this is not the time to be comparing yourself with other people or wondering whether you should have a different attitude to pain. You have a job to do, which is to recover from your illness and get home; this will happen more quickly if your pain is minimised.

If you are in pain (as opposed to feeling slight discomfort), you must tell your doctor or nurse. You should not 'be brave', suffer in silence or feel that you should not bother busy staff. This is not helpful for the following reasons:

Good pain relief is important for general well-being. It reduces suffering and helps you recover more quickly.

Pain control helps reduce complications. For example, if you can breathe deeply and cough easily after an operation, you are less likely to develop a chest infection.

If you can move around easily, you can stay active and are less likely to get blood clots. Your muscles will not weaken as much, which will reduce the need for rehabilitation and allow you to be discharged more promptly.

It is easier to treat pain before it becomes too severe. It is therefore best to ask for pain relief as soon as you feel any pain, rather than waiting for it to get worse.

Occasionally, pain is a warning sign that a serious problem has developed. You must let staff know immediately if your pain changes and/or becomes more severe. This will allow any serious problems to be identified quickly.

How pain is treated

Pain management is now a highly developed form of medicine and many hospitals have specialist pain management teams. A typical pain management team is made up of nurse specialists and anaesthetists, who work closely with other professionals such as physiotherapists and pharmacists. If you have pain that is unresponsive to standard treatments, you may therefore be referred to this team. They may visit you at your bed or you may attend a special pain clinic.

The World Health Organization has described an 'analgesic ladder', which nicely captures the approach now taken to pain management. Staff will begin with simple pain treatments, but can go higher up the ladder if you need more help. To begin with, simple analgesics such as paracetamol will be prescribed. If this is not sufficient, something stronger such as codeine or dihydrocodeine may be used. If your pain is partly due to inflammation, you may be prescribed an anti-inflammatory drug such as ibuprofen or naproxen if these are suitable for you. Often more than one drug is given, such as paracetamol plus an anti-inflammatory drug, or paracetamol plus codeine, as they work in different ways and provide better pain relief when combined. If the pain is more severe, there are many other options, including stronger medication such as morphine, and there are different ways of administering pain relief (see Table 5).

Table 5 Ways of giving pain relief

Types of pain relief	How they work
Capsules, tablets or liquids to swallow	Capsules, tablets and liquids are used for all types of pain. They usually take about 15 to 20 minutes to work and may be prescribed to be taken regularly, or on a 'when required' basis.
Injections	Injections may be given through a cannula (a short plastic tube) into your vein (intravenous) or into your leg or buttock muscle (intramuscular) using a fine needle. Injections into a vein start to work within two to three minutes. Injections given into your muscle take a little longer to work.
Suppositories	A suppository is a small waxy pellet which is placed in your bottom. The pellet dissolves and the medication is absorbed into your body. Suppositories are useful if you cannot swallow or if you feel sick and might vomit. Some are aimed at helping you open your bowels, and some pain relief medication is most effective when given in this manner. Usually, suppositories take about 30 minutes to work.
Intravenous infusions	This method of pain relief uses a machine that continuously infuses a strong painkiller into a cannula in your vein. The amount of

Continued ...

Continued from previous page

	painkiller is controlled by the nurse looking after you. This method may be used for one to two days after an operation.
Patient-controlled analgesia ('PCA')	Pain relief is delivered via a machine controlled by you, the patient. A pump which contains a drug such as morphine (a strong painkiller) is linked to a handset which has a button. When you press the button, you receive a dose of the painkiller into a cannula in your vein. The painkiller will work within two to three minutes. The pump will be set up in such a way that it 'locks-out' for a short period after each administration. This prevents you from giving yourself an overdose.
Regional anaesthesia	This involves numbing a specific part of your body. Epidural analgesia is a type of regional anaesthesia. If you agree, your anaesthetist may decide to insert a catheter (a long, fine plastic tube) into your back, which will stay in place for up to three days. Medication is delivered continuously through the catheter to provide adequate pain relief to the part of your body affected. This provides very effective pain relief, but also means that you cannot easily move that part of your body. Other regional 'blocks' make a whole arm or leg feel numb, giving excellent pain control after bone or joint surgery.

Sometimes you may be prescribed a pain medicine which you can ask for just when you need it, rather than being given it regularly. You may hear staff referring to this as 'when required', or 'PRN' medication. PRN stands for *pro re nata*, a Latin phrase which means 'as the circumstances require'. You may want to ask if you have any additional pain relief prescribed to be given 'when required', so that you know you can ask for it if you need it.

Tell the staff if you are feeling worse

Hospital staff are skilled at specialist investigations, diagnoses and treatments. They also have to be good at detecting problems and reacting quickly to them, which is rather different to being technically skilled. It is more a matter of watching patients carefully, checking vital signs regularly, anticipating possible problems and above all listening to patients and relatives. You can help, whether as a patient or a relative, by telling hospital staff if you feel the condition is getting worse.

While in hospital you should generally have your observations ('vital signs') measured at least every 12 hours. They are called vital signs because they are a good indicator of a person's state of health. A nurse or healthcare assistant will check your pulse (heart rate), temperature and blood pressure, and ask if you are in pain; they may check your breathing and how much oxygen is in your blood. As well as recording the signs, they should also look at you generally and get a sense of how you are. The nurses or doctors may decide you need these checks and observations more or less often as your condition progresses. If your vital signs are not being monitored at all, you should ask why this is the case.

Your pulse, blood pressure and other vital signs change during the day; minor fluctuations are perfectly normal. The staff are looking for more substantial changes, such as a steadily rising or falling blood pressure. To help them assess when changes may indicate a deterioration in your condition, the staff often use a system called an 'early warning score' or a similar name.

The score is calculated on a paper chart or on a computer and assesses the overall change in your vital signs. If you are becoming unwell, your score increases and indicates that staff need to take some action:

A small increase in your score might indicate a problem but could just be a temporary change. In this case the nurse in charge will be told and your observations may be checked more frequently until they return to normal levels.

If the changes in your vital signs suggest there might be a serious problem, a senior nurse or a doctor will come to investigate the reasons for these changes. They will then decide what further actions are needed.

Most hospitals have a 'critical care outreach' team who provide expert support for nurses and doctors on the wards. This team may be asked to come and check on you if your condition seems to be getting worse.

Your friends or family should also tell staff if they feel your condition is getting worse. They need to explain as clearly and firmly as possible what they have noticed: 'When we came yesterday, she was sleepy but calm and talking to us. Today she seems confused and is hot and sweating …' Your family or friends should:

- first talk to the staff and explain why they are concerned;
- ask staff to explain what observations are being carried out and ask what the patient's early warning score is;
- ask for a senior nurse or doctor to be called if they are still concerned.

Feeling anxious or stressed

We all know what it is like to feel anxious. Going to the dentist, taking an exam, speaking in public and experiencing sudden turbulence when flying are all situations which make many of us anxious. Once they are over, though, we calm down and quickly return to normal. Our heart rate and breathing slow down again, we stop sweating, and that nasty feeling in the pit of the stomach fades away. A degree of anxiety in a challenging situation is normal and useful in that it makes us alert and ready for a challenge. However, when anxiety lasts a long time, it has the opposite effect; we feel increasingly stressed, overwhelmed with problems and less able to cope.

You can recognise stress in yourself (or in someone else) by being aware of how you feel, the thoughts you are having and your behaviour. Common physical responses to stress include a pounding heart, short and fast breathing, a dry mouth and clammy hands. Your muscles may feel tense, and while you may feel tired, getting to sleep may be difficult. Rapid breathing can reduce the carbon dioxide in your blood, leading to tingling and numbness in the hands, feet and lips. This scares some people, which worsens the situation further. Common mental and emotional responses include feeling anxious and worried, being irritable and on-edge, thoughts racing through your mind that you cannot control, and a feeling of being overwhelmed even by simple problems.

Feeling stressed and anxious can be very unpleasant. Sometimes the symptoms are strong and people believe that they are physically ill. If someone's heart is pounding and they are sweating, they may think 'I must be having a heart attack', but it is often due to anxiety. There are many things you can do to help yourself (see Box 26), but if you find that you are feeling very anxious for most of the day you need to tell the staff looking after you. As with pain, it is much easier for them to help you early on and then monitor how you are feeling than to be called when you are incredibly anxious. Sometimes just talking your worries over with a nurse, doctor or other member of staff will be all the reassurance you need. You may be worried about a particular symptom and they can tell you that this is perfectly

Box 26 *Dealing with stress in hospital*

- Bring in familiar objects such as family photographs, books or pillows.

- Listen to relaxing music during procedures. Bring in a radio or music player with headphones, or ask a visitor to bring one in for you.

- Do not be afraid to ask for what you need. If you are cold, ask for another blanket. If you cannot sleep, tell the nurse. If appropriate, they may ask a doctor to prescribe a sleeping tablet for you.

- Ask not to be disturbed when you want to rest.

- Be positive in the way you talk to yourself: 'Hundreds of people have coped well with this test and so will I.'

- Take your mind off the problem by using distraction — read a magazine, listen to music. Remember that laughter can be a very effective method of relieving stress.

- If you are unclear about the nature of the procedure you are going to have, ask one of the nurses to explain what will happen.

- If you are afraid, talk to a member of the ward staff. They should be able to reassure you and you may find that your fears are groundless.

- Many hospital patients derive great comfort from speaking to a chaplain. If you would like to speak to the chaplain, you only have to ask.

normal and will pass in a day or two. However, if necessary you can also be prescribed medication to help you sleep or to control your anxiety. For more serious mental health problems, counsellors and psychologists may be available, as well as psychiatrists (doctors who specialise in treating mental health problems).

I just need someone to talk to ...

Many people are lucky enough to have regular visits from family and friends while they are in hospital. Some people, though, may not have family or friends nearby and may not have anyone to share their worries and fears. You may also want to talk about matters that are difficult to express to family members. You may feel that your family just does not understand how you feel, or you may be concerned about 'burdening them' with your concerns. People who are seriously ill may feel that they will not recover and may be fearful for both themselves and their families. Illness may also provoke a crisis of faith, as you question your beliefs and the way you have lived your life up to now.

In such circumstances, it can be very useful to talk to some-one who is sympathetic but not directly involved either with your life or your treatment. Clinical staff, such as nurses and doctors, are generally too busy to talk for prolonged periods, but they can contact other staff who can help you. Counsellors and others can offer such a service, and the hospital chaplaincy can be a par-ticularly useful source of support. They are simply there for you, to listen and to offer what guidance they can. Many people are supported by their faith in times of crisis, and chaplains regard spiritual resources as being equally important to our personal courage and resilience. In the UK many chaplains are Christian, but other faiths will also be represented. In any case chaplains are there for all patients, and indeed all staff, no matter what the person's faith or whether they have any faith at all. The chaplain will not ask you when you last went to a church, synagogue, temple or mosque before agreeing to see you!

Chaplains can provide the opportunity for individual prayer. They can arrange religious ceremonies when requested (includ-ing weddings!), and can arrange for representatives of other

faith communities to visit as appropriate. However, they also try
to think about the whole person, which includes not only spiritual matters but also your social and emotional well-being. They
will be able, for instance, to discuss how your illness has affected
your family relationships, your worries about returning to work,
or a feeling that you will never return to being the person you
were before your illness. Help in crisis situations, including relationship problems and bereavement care, are all regular areas of
chaplaincy involvement. Chaplains can talk to family members as
well as patients during times of crisis.

If you want to see the chaplain, just ask a member of the
hospital staff to contact them on your behalf. Alternatively, you
can telephone the chaplain's office or go there yourself. The hospital website will have information on chaplaincy and counselling
services, or staff can provide the details. Outside office hours a
chaplain is usually available on call to visit a patient in an emergency; in these circumstances, a member of hospital staff would
need to make the request.

Problems with care and treatment

We are very much aware that hospital care does not always
meet the standard that we hope for, and that problems of many
kinds – large and small – can arise during and after a hospital
stay. Throughout this book we have encouraged you to speak
to the staff whenever you have any concerns; this is almost
always the right thing to do in the first instance. But suppose
you feel that the staff are not listening or have not understood
your worries? Or perhaps you feel you have been treated
disrespectfully or you are concerned about standards on the
ward? This is when you can turn to other sources of advice,
such as the Patient Advice and Liaison Service (PALS) in
English hospitals; the Community Health Council in Wales; the
Patient Advice and Support Service (PASS), which is delivered

by the Scottish Citizens Advice Bureau (CAB) in Scotland; or the Patient and Client Council in Northern Ireland. All healthcare organisations, NHS and private, will have an individual or a department that you can go to with any concerns.

These departments were set up to help patients, and their relatives and carers, find a speedy and effective solution to any problems they may encounter. Their purpose is to:

- provide an easy-access, confidential service to assist patients, relatives and carers;
- offer on-the-spot advice and information if you have queries or difficulties;
- listen to your concerns and help you find ways of resolving them;
- act as a point of contact for all those wishing to get advice and information about hospital services and other health information.

You will find information about the PALS or equivalent service advertised throughout the hospital. Often their office will be near the main reception. You can either visit in person or telephone. If you contact PALS for assistance or advice, they usually guarantee to contact you in person within 24 hours of your request or by the next working day. They will then discuss the issue you have raised and advise you of the best way to resolve it. PALS staff will talk to you in complete confidence, and will only pass on information to other people if you give them permission; they can talk to family or friends, but also only with the patient's permission. The PALS team can act on your behalf if you wish. For instance, they can contact the hospital catering management team about the food you are receiving or speak to a doctor about a clinical matter that is concerning you. They can also advise you on how to make a formal complaint about any serious issues and, if you do not get a satisfactory response, how to contact the Independent Complaints Advocacy Service. They will not pass on your details without your permission, so you should not be concerned that raising a complaint will affect your future care.

CHAPTER TWENTY-TWO

Visiting and supporting others

Visiting a friend or relative in hospital is an important part of helping them to feel better and adjust to a new situation. Visits and other support from family and friends can keep patients' spirits up and encourage them to recover and return to normal life. This chapter considers what you can do to help a friend or relative while they are in hospital, and how the hospital staff will accommodate this.

Who can visit?

In general, any adult family members, friends, colleagues or neighbours can visit as long as the patient agrees. Children can usually visit with the permission of the ward manager, but must be closely supervised. Some hospitals may suggest that children under a certain age do not visit because it is difficult for them to appreciate the need to be quiet. The hospital environment can also sometimes be distressing or confusing, so it is best to ask the ward staff in advance if you wish to bring young children to the ward.

While visitors are welcome, staff will ask you to respect the other patients in the ward by being reasonably quiet and not disturbing patients who are trying to rest. There is likely to be a limit to the number of visitors allowed at any one time (usually two), so do check with the ward staff if three or more people want to visit together. Please also switch your mobile telephone to a silent setting.

People in hospital are often very tired. They will appreciate your visit, but they may become exhausted quite quickly. Short, frequent visits of about 20 minutes may be better than one long visit. As people recover, though, they can get quite bored while waiting to go home; then a longer visit with lively conversation may be very welcome. Here, a patient talks about her experience.

....

I was in hospital for about a week and felt fairly well during most of that time, but I had to be monitored closely so wasn't allowed home. My husband was working long hours and my wider family lived hundreds of miles away. I wasn't particularly ill, so there wasn't any reason for them to visit. I was in a single room, which was great for privacy, but I felt bored, lonely and generally fed up. So when friends came to visit one evening, bringing magazines, some treats to eat and, most of all, some lively conversation it really transformed my day. When I've been really unwell I only wanted close family to visit, but once feeling better I think it's great to have friends come in and cheer you up!

....

Before you visit

If you need to find out which ward your friend or relative is on, you can call the hospital in advance or ask at the main desk when you arrive. The receptionist should be able to find where they are, and tell you how to get there.

If at all possible, ask your friend or relative before you visit and let them know when you are coming. This prevents too many visitors turning up at the same time, and also allows the patient to let you know if they do not feel well enough to see you on that particular day.

Most wards or units in the hospital will have set visiting hours. This is because hospitals are busy places and there is a great deal to do during the day, particularly in the early stages of someone's hospital stay. Patients need to have investigations, receive treatment, see their nurses and doctors, and also have enough time to eat and rest. Visiting hours also protect the welfare and privacy of all the patients on the ward and allow them to get some rest outside visiting hours. Many wards operate a system of 'protected meal times' to ensure that people in hospital can eat their meals without being interrupted. During these times visitors are not generally permitted and even hospital staff do not see patients unless it is really essential.

Visiting hours for children in hospital or people who are very sick will usually be more flexible. If it is simply not possible for you to visit during the usual visiting hours, telephone the ward and ask to speak to the ward manager or nurse in charge that day to arrange a convenient time. Hospital staff will try to make special arrangements for people who have to travel a long way or who are caring for children or other dependents.

Keeping the patient and yourself safe

Hospital patients are usually more susceptible to infections than the general public. Transmission of infection is one of the most significant dangers faced by people in hospital, so if you are ill err on the side of caution and ask the nurses whether you should visit. You should certainly not visit if you have suffered from diarrhoea or vomiting within the last 48 hours or if you have any other infectious conditions, from a nasty common cold to an illness like chicken pox.

When visiting, always clean your hands on the way into the ward and again when you leave. You will find alcohol gel dispensers near the entry to the wards, in the patient's room and at other points in the hospital. This alcohol gel disinfects your hands; it is very quick and easy to put on your hands and rub in. More details are given in Chapter 19.

Infections can easily be transmitted on the ward, even by healthy visitors. For this reason:

- you should not put your feet on a patient's bed;
- you should avoid touching a patient's wound or any of the equipment that might be attached to them;
- you must use the visitors' toilets, never the patients' toilets;
- you must not share tissues or towels with patients.

Smoking is banned in hospitals, so do not smoke anywhere in the hospital or its grounds, unless there is a specific designated smoking area. People who are feeling ill or taking certain drugs may find the smell of tobacco or strong perfume quite nauseating, even if these smells would not normally bother them.

What can I bring in?

If someone is in hospital for a planned operation or investigation, they are likely to have brought in their clothes and other things that they needed for their stay. You may be able to speak to them before your visit to see what else they might like. If you cannot speak to them, look at the list in Chapter 18 (Box 21) which suggests things that make people feel more comfortable in hospital.

If someone was admitted as an emergency, they may not have anything with them. In this case, you should consider bringing clothes, toiletries, their mobile phone, their glasses or hearing aid, books, magazines and anything else that you know they would appreciate. It is also important to bring in any medical information that might help the hospital staff. This includes a list of the patient's medication, their prescriptions, copies of any hospital letters, and the name, address and phone number of their GP.

In general, you should avoid bringing in expensive items or things that cannot be replaced if lost. However, a few familiar items can help people feel at home, especially if they are in hospital for a long while. Photographs, or letters or drawings by grandchildren or younger relatives, can be a source of real joy and comfort. You can bring food, drinks and sweets into the hospital, but most wards ask you not to bring food that needs to be reheated; they may not have a microwave and such food can pose an infection risk.

Asking questions

If you want to ask about your friend's or relative's progress and how they are feeling, always ask them first provided they are feeling well enough to explain. However, you may find that they do not actually want to discuss their illness and would rather talk about other things. This may be because they are anxious or embarrassed or because their problems are still being investigated and they do not have a definitive diagnosis. On occasion it is simply that they are fed up with talking about their illness and would much rather hear about friends and family outside the hospital! We suggest that you are guided by the patient and follow their wishes.

If you wish to speak to a member of staff about your friend or relative, it is best to approach the nurse looking after them. Remember that staff will only provide information about a patient's progress and condition to relatives or friends if the patient has given their permission first. This is to protect people's right to confidentiality. If you telephone, staff are usually happy to give general information about how the patient is feeling but will not discuss their condition in any detail unless they know that the patient has specifically agreed for them to do so.

When this is the case, nursing staff will be able to discuss the patient's progress and explain the investigations and treatment they are having. However, you may sometimes need to have a more detailed discussion with a doctor to find out more. Arranging a time to meet with a more senior doctor can require a little flexibility, as other duties such as clinics or operating lists are fixed in their timetables. Another option is to arrange for the doctor to telephone you. Where possible, to avoid confusion, we recommend that one member of the family should be the main point of contact and act as a link to everyone else.

If a patient is too unwell to make a decision as to whether or not information about them can be shared with their friends and family, this will be discussed with their next of kin. There is a legal framework which staff will use to protect the confidentiality of patients while also trying to address the fears and concerns of loved ones.

Visiting people on a hospital ward

The layouts of wards vary, but there will usually be a mixture of shared 'bays' (each accommodating several patients) and single rooms ('side rooms'). The bays are now nearly always kept single gender to maintain privacy and dignity for all patients. There will usually be a nurses' station, where the hospital staff can make phone calls and update their documentation, and a small room for more private conversations. Wards will often have locked doors, especially outside visiting hours, and you will need to ring a buzzer or intercom to request entry.

In the shared bays, beds will be separated by curtains. The curtains are used to maintain patients' privacy when they are being examined, washed or having minor procedures performed. If the curtains are closed, you should not enter.

The type of bed and mattress the patient is using may also vary, as some patients need special air mattresses to help protect their skin. Some patients have rails on their beds to prevent them falling out of bed. These are only used in certain circumstances and most hospitals will have a policy to help decide who needs them. All patients will have a chair by their bed; if they are well enough, they will be encouraged to get out of bed and sit in the chair as much as possible, to maintain posture and core strength, and to help with breathing.

Visiting people in the intensive care unit

Visiting someone in the intensive care unit (ICU) can be a rather upsetting experience. You will, of course, be worried about your friend or relative and you may also find intensive care an unsettling environment. We will explain some of the most important points here, but you may also like to read the chapter about intensive care (Chapter 9).

You may be shocked by your first sight of your loved one when they are in an ICU. Patients in the ICU are very unwell, and will often be attached to a number of special machines. They may be kept unconscious (with a general anaesthetic), or at least heavily sedated, for the first few days to lessen their distress and allow these machines to support their recovery. They may therefore not respond to your voice or touch. They will have a number of wires and tubes attached to their body. You will see a monitor showing the patterns of their breathing, their pulse and blood pressure.

Patients in the ICU usually have an individual nurse allocated to them, who is with them almost all the time. The nurse can explain how the patient is, whether they have woken up at all, what treatment is being given, and when they are expected to leave intensive care. They can arrange for you to see a doctor if you need to have a more detailed discussion.

You will be allowed to sit at the bedside and hold the patient's hand, just as you would on a ward. You should talk to the patient as much or as little as you like; they may sense that you are there even if you do not get any response. Do not be afraid to just sit in silence and hold their hand.

Visiting is the best thing you can do to help

We are aware that this chapter contains a lot of dos and don'ts, and hope that it has not come across as simply a list of forbidding instructions! This information is important, as it helps protect both the person in hospital and their visitors. However, please do not worry about visiting. Hospital staff understand that visits from friends and family help patients enormously, and support their recovery and return home. The staff are there to help you as well as their patients. If you are worried about what you can or cannot do, just ask. The main thing is to be there for your loved one.

Specific
circumstances

CHAPTER TWENTY-THREE

Children in hospital

A child's admission to hospital is almost always worrying. As a parent, grandparent or carer, you and the child are likely to find this an uncertain and stressful time. For children, hospital can be an unfamiliar environment, with strange equipment, new sounds and smells, and unfamiliar people. For parents, family members or carers, this is a time of disruption at work as well as at home. You may also be witnessing suffering and distress in a child or young person whom you love.

Children and teenagers tend to become unwell, and also recover, more quickly than adults. Children are different from adults in their understanding, their emotions, their relationships and their physical development. Their bodies are obviously smaller than those of adults and this often presents challenges for those caring for them. However, illness in a child may also appear in a different form to the same illness in an adult, and children may react very differently to drugs and other treatments. Because children are different from adults in so many ways, hospitals that treat children have specific paediatric teams who specialise in looking after them.

Children may have almost any of the investigations and treatments described in the other chapters of this book, although some would be very unusual for a child. If your child is in hospital, it will be helpful to read other relevant chapters. In this chapter, we provide some additional information that is particularly relevant to children.

The paediatric team

The paediatric staff have the same grades and titles as the staff looking after adult patients (see Chapter 7), but they special- ise in looking after children. The medical team on a children's ward will consist of paediatric consultants and their teams of junior doctors. There will also be a team of paediatric nurses, one or more paediatric pharmacists, and a dedicated group of therapists for children: dieticians, physiotherapists, speech and language therapists and occupational therapists. You may also encounter doctors from other specialties, most often the surgical and orthopaedic (bones and fractures) teams, who may or may not be exclusively children's doctors. A senior surgeon who looks after adults will be called a consultant surgeon, but if they look after children they will be called a consultant paediatric surgeon.

The paediatric clinical teams will work in shifts. Over a 24-hour period, two or three different teams will look after your child. For example, the doctor who admits your child from the emergency department may be different from the one who takes care of them on the ward. The teams of nurses and doctors have for- mal handover meetings to make sure that the team going home passes on all important information to the new team taking over. However, you may still find that you need to tell your child's story more than once when seeing different professionals during their stay. You should always feel able to ask the names of members of staff, or ask them to explain their role in the team, so that you can keep track of who is looking after your child.

A child's admission to hospital

Children can be admitted to hospital by a number of different routes. These include attendance at an emergency department, admission directly to a children's ward – with a new medical problem or a worsening of an old one – or a planned medical or surgical admission for a procedure or assessment. Rarely, a child may require admission to a paediatric intensive care unit (PICU) if they are very unwell; if they are only recently born, this may be the neonatal intensive care unit (NICU). The hospital itself may be a local hospital, or a more specialised hospital or unit just for children. Some of these are entities in their own right, like Great Ormond Street Hospital in London and Alder Hey Children's Hospital in Liverpool, and some are located within major teaching hospitals, such as the University Hospital of Wales in Cardiff and the Royal Hospital for Sick Children in Edinburgh.

Children and teenagers can become sick very rapidly. Here is one mother's experience of a sudden emergency.

....

I heard an unusual noise, ran upstairs and found my daughter fitting in her cot. The paramedics arrived and handled us very professionally. Our assessment and admission to the children's ward seemed very fast. Once there, despite feeling at sea in this unfamiliar environment, I felt confident that she was in the right place and I trusted their judgement. I guess this is what I needed most from the medical team, who were people I didn't know. The nurses were superb with us – they made our stay in hospital easier, and allowed us to stay close to her 24/7. I don't recall ever being asked to step out, or feeling I was in the way. When we'd settled in, I felt awfully guilty; I thought about my being downstairs at home marking students' essays and her being upstairs alone, even though I heard the sound of the fitting and acted immediately. Once the diagnosis of febrile convulsion had been made, I felt that we should have seen it ourselves! It was a huge relief to receive the reassurance that this wasn't uncommon in children and that it didn't mean a lifetime problem. This was invaluable and gave me huge confidence.

....

Because illnesses may be sudden, the decision to admit a child to hospital, and decisions made during the admission, may also be made very quickly. You may find it hard to keep up with the pace of events and the process can seem quite confusing. As soon as possible you should ask for some time with your child's consultant or another member of the medical team to discuss progress and ask what they think is causing your child's symptoms. They may have been able to make a diagnosis already, and will give you a clear explanation of what is happening and what treatment is being given. On other occasions, they may still be investigating the problem and not yet be able to give you a firm answer. The team will always be honest with you, so do not think that they are holding information back. Assessing and treating children, especially very young children, is difficult. You may have to wait until the situation is clearer.

The children's ward

Hospitals care for children separately from adults. Most hospitals have a separate children's emergency department with its own waiting-room and paediatric staff. Children's wards are usually colourful and child-orientated, with plenty of pictures on the walls, toys, a playroom and a hospital school. The ward will probably have some open bays containing several beds and some individual rooms or cubicles. The individual rooms are normally reserved for children who are very ill or who pose a risk to other children because they have an infection or are too young to have received any vaccinations. There are usually no restrictions at all on visiting times for parents, who can be with their child throughout the day and night. However, there are usually some restrictions for other visitors in order to protect children's sleeping and eating times.

For teenagers, the children's ward, with its toys and play area, may not be an ideal environment. Larger hospitals may have dedicated adolescent units, but most local hospitals do not admit enough teenagers to make this possible. Staff try to provide age-appropriate reading, films and schoolwork for adolescents and young people, and try to place them in ward bays together rather than with younger children.

Paediatric wards usually have a ward round each morning and sometimes a second one later in the day. These are the times when the medical team visit each patient to assess their progress, examine them, talk to families, and make a plan for their ongoing treatment and then discharge from hospital. The ward round is an ideal time for parents to hear more about their child's progress, and to bring the medical staff up to date with their own impressions and knowledge of their child. Ask the nurses for the timings of ward rounds so that you can be available when your child is discussed.

Looking after your child in hospital

The family unit supporting the child is a unique source of strength and power for both the child and the medical team looking after them. The family can provide practical care, support and love for the child. The family is also a source of information and in-depth knowledge for the medical team. Support from the family is particularly crucial when a child is discharged from hospital but may still need further treatment at home.

Children's wards always have space for parents to stay. At least one of you will be able to be with your child all the time and there may be space for both of you to sleep near your child. There may be brief occasions when you are temporarily separated from your child, such as when your child is first taken to the intensive care unit or an operating theatre, but staff will work hard to keep this to a minimum.

You may have dropped everything to bring your child to hospital, and may not have been expecting an overnight admission. If your child is admitted for a few days, you will have time to collect clothes, toiletries and toys from home. Children are usually able to wear their own clothes in hospital and this helps to lessen the unfamiliarity of the experience. However, clothing and nappies can be provided for you by the children's ward if they are needed immediately after admission. Car parking may require payment, but ward staff may be able to provide you with a special parking permit intended for the parents of children who are ill.

Box 27 *Practical ways to support your child*

- Keep a note of the consultant who is overseeing your child's care, and if possible the names of the junior doctors involved. This makes it much easier to find the right person if you have questions or need more information.

- Ask the nurses about the ward visiting times, the process for staying overnight with your child, the ward telephone number, and whether they can give you a parking permit.

- Ask when the ward rounds take place so that you can be there when the team discusses your child.

- Ask who you should speak to on the ward if you are worried about anything. Your child will usually have a dedicated nurse who is the ideal person to talk to and discuss any concerns with.

- Bring familiar toys, games or activities, food and clothes for your child or teenager.

- Where possible, keep copies of the discharge letters, appointments and results to form a personal medical record for your child. This can be a useful way of remembering what has happened, and can be invaluable in any subsequent admission to hospital until the full medical notes become available.

- Ask for a doctor's note or discharge letter if you need this to explain your child's absence from school.

Box 27 lists practical ways in which you can support your child. To make the hospital stay as easy as possible for them, you may wish to bring in toys, books or games. You will be amazed at children's abilities to play even when they are very unwell. Boredom and unfamiliar environments can make a child even more unhappy than they are as a result of their illness; home comforts, toys and games can really help. The children's ward will have a play area, where your child can mix with other children or play with a parent. For older children, there is often a teenagers' room, or an area to which younger children do not have access, so that older children can relax and be with their peers. Occasionally a child will not be allowed to mix with other children because of the risk of infection, but you will be told if your child needs to be separated from others.

The hospital will provide food for children and their parents, with some choice and flexibility. You may prefer to bring particular foods for your child, especially if your baby or toddler prefers a particular formula milk. Ask the ward staff where you can store food, and what kind of food and drink your child can have. There are times, usually before surgery, when your child will not be allowed to eat or drink for a few hours; if in doubt, ask the doctors or nurses whether this applies to your child. The ward will probably also have an area where parents can make coffee and tea. This may be behind a locked door to make sure that children do not gain entry and accidentally hurt themselves.

Communication is essential

Young children can be remarkably good communicators and a skilled doctor will be able to find out a great deal about their problems by talking to them. However, you obviously understand how to communicate with your child better than anyone. If your child needs help, do not hesitate to guide the medical team in the best way to communicate with them.

Diagnosing and treating babies and very young children who are not yet able to talk is obviously more difficult, even when parents are there to help. It can be challenging for the medical team to diagnose the underlying problem when the child is unable to explain how they feel or where it hurts. The process of diagnosis and developing a full understanding of the problem may therefore take time. This can be a frustrating time for parents, as they wait for more tests and observations before a diagnosis is made and treatment is started.

For teenagers and young people, the loss of independence and control in the hospital environment can be quite disturbing; families can be vital to the process of ensuring that their voices are heard and that they get care appropriate to their needs. Doctors and nurses know that it is essential to talk directly to teenagers, and to engage them in the decision-making process just as they would with adults. However, they also appreciate that parental support and guidance will be needed if a teenage patient prefers this, or is too ill to make decisions. In some cases, it may be necessary for medical teams to talk to older children alone to discuss the situation and ask for their personal views. This is quite usual, and is part of understanding how best to help them. Open communication and honesty between the medical team and teenagers is critical if young patients are to take an active and proper part in the decision-making process and the ongoing management of their health.

Consent to treatment

Young children are legally considered to lack the ability to consent formally to their own treatment, or to refuse it. They can, of course, express their views; every parent will want to listen carefully to what their child says, and understand their wishes and any fears. However, in the end the child's parent or guardian will be asked to provide consent for treatment – although in an emergency doctors may act in the best interests of the child to provide life-saving care without having obtained consent in advance.

A young child's inability to fully understand the implications of their illness and the benefits of treatment may also lead to conflict when a child is distressed by having to undergo a procedure, such as providing a blood sample or taking a medicine. This can be upsetting for parents to witness and may leave parents feeling responsible for the unpleasant experience or angry with the medical team. Older children will have developed a greater understanding and their views on the proposed treatment options always need to be considered. As always, you should ask questions in order to reassure yourself that the investigation and treatment, even if it is unpleasant, is in the best interests of your child.

Keeping in touch with home and school

Children in hospital miss out on school and on time with friends and family. Missing a short period of school is unlikely to cause any problems in the longer term. However, for a longer hospital stay it is worth talking to your child's teachers to obtain some appropriate schoolwork to do while they are recovering. The unavoidable disruption to school caused by an admission to hospital can be partly offset by involvement with the hospital school. Even smaller paediatric units in local hospitals usually have a dedicated schoolteacher and schoolroom, with age-appropriate activities and learning opportunities for children and teenagers once they are well enough. These are usually flexible and fun activities aiming to address some of the children's educational needs while they are in hospital.

Children in hospital, like adults, should be encouraged to stay in touch with friends and family as much as possible throughout their stay. Parents may be able to stay with the child for much of the time, but inevitably there will be times when this is not possible due to other family and work commitments. At these times visits from other children, including siblings, can form a bridge and a continued link with daily life, so that the sick child does not feel isolated from friends and school. For older teenagers, social media are likely to be a big part of their life; they can remain glued to their mobile phones in hospital just as they are at home!

Looking after yourself

Having a child in hospital is worrying but also potentially exhausting. If your child is very young or seriously ill, you will naturally want to be with them at all times. However, once they are stable it may not be sensible to spend every minute with them. Other friends and family members can take turns while you go home to rest. Remember to look after yourself as well as your child. Even very young children intuitively sense when their parents are stressed and exhausted, and if you can look after yourself it will help them to feel confident and secure.

CHAPTER TWENTY-FOUR

Older people in hospital

The majority of patients in hospital are over 65 years of age; most people will be admitted to hospital at some point during their older years. Most of this book is relevant to older and younger adults alike, but in this chapter we focus specifically on those who are very old and perhaps less actively involved in their own care. It is particularly written for the families, carers and friends of older people – and for anyone else who may wish to understand their care and to support them during a hospital stay.

Going into hospital can be frightening for those who are very old. Even if the older person has had previous admissions, it can be a worrying time both for them and for those who love and care for them. Healthcare for older people is not always as straightforward as for younger people. It can present unique challenges, particularly as older people often have many complex problems that can interact with one another.

What makes a hospital stay different for older people?

Older people are commonly admitted to hospital as an emergency, following a sudden illness such as a fall, infection, heart attack or stroke; they may also, of course, be admitted for planned procedures or operations. Older people frequently have a number of long-term conditions, such as high blood pressure, heart disease, diabetes or dementia. As people get older and have more medical conditions, they become more vulnerable to illness generally and less able to live independently; this is sometimes referred to as 'frailty'. An important consequence of frailty is that an illness may have a greater and longer-lasting impact on an older person in comparison to the same illness in someone younger and fitter. The hospital stay can be longer and more complex because of pre-existing problems and because each treatment may need to be carefully adjusted so that the older person has the maximum benefit from it. Being frail also means that the person may be more sensitive to the side-effects of certain treatments, and may be more at risk of things going wrong.

The multidisciplinary team caring for older people

Most hospitals will have teams of specialists in older people's care, who will either take over the patient's care very early on in their admission or provide advice to the surgical or medical team looking after them. These specialist older people's teams focus on identifying and managing common problems, maximising mobility and function, and overseeing discharge planning. Older people who have a single problem that requires specialist services, such as those of a cardiology or surgical team, will generally go to the appropriate ward to have that problem treated. However, older people who have several medical problems and more complex needs are generally best treated on a specialist 'medicine for the elderly' ward.

The team will be led by a senior doctor, who is usually referred to as either a consultant in elderly medicine or a consultant geriatrician. It will include doctors, nurses, physiotherapists, occupational therapists, dieticians, speech and swallowing therapists, pharmacists, discharge coordinators and social workers (see Chapter 7 for explanations of these roles). All will be experienced in the specific needs of older people and they will work together to help the patient recover from their illness, get them as mobile and independent as possible, and arrange care and support after hospital as needed.

Dementia and delirium

Dementia, which causes problems with memory and the ability to carry out tasks, is common among older people. Dementia is caused when the brain is damaged by diseases such as Alzheimer's disease or a series of strokes. Dementia is progressive, which means that the symptoms generally get worse over time. When a person with dementia is admitted to hospital, the strange environment and different routines can make their symptoms worse.

When an older person becomes acutely unwell with any physical condition, they may experience sudden confusion and loss of their mental function; this is known as delirium and can be associated with a loss of ability to concentrate, drowsiness or agitation. This is common, affecting around a third of older people in hospital; it is often the reason for admission to hospital in the first place, but can also happen during the hospital stay. Delirium can be frightening, for the patient and for their family or carers. Strategies to improve and prevent it include ensuring that the older person is well hydrated, avoiding constipation and problems with bladder-emptying, and ensuring that hearing aids and glasses are worn if required. People usually recover from delirium, but may take some time to do so.

Consent and capacity

As explained in Chapter 10, patients in hospital need to give their consent for any investigations or treatment. Except in special circumstances – such as emergencies – hospital staff are not permitted to carry out any investigation or procedure without the patient's consent. People are entitled to refuse treatment if they do not think it is in their best interests.

However, there are some circumstances when people are not able to make decisions themselves. This could be because they are unconscious, because they have dementia or some other mental health problem, or for a variety of other reasons. In England and Wales, the Mental Capacity Act 2005 sets out the legal framework and procedures to be followed in these circumstances. If someone is unable to consent to the proposed treatment, a doctor must act in their best interests. It is not possible for a relative to give consent on someone else's behalf, but the doctor is expected to consult relatives about the patient's likely wishes. If your relative cannot give consent, a doctor may therefore ask you to help decide the most appropriate course of action. You may know from previous conversations what the patient would decide if they were able to express their views about a particular course of treatment. If significant medical treatment is proposed and someone has no family or friends to support them, medical staff must appoint an independent mental capacity advocate to represent the patient's interests. Similarly, the Adults with Incapacity (Scotland) Act 2000 sets out in law a range of options to help people aged 16 or over who lack the capacity to make some or all decisions for themselves. There is currently no equivalent law on mental capacity in Northern Ireland.

Looking after older people in hospital

The suggestions and advice in other sections of the book on looking after yourself and on receiving support from family are important for anyone in hospital (see Chapters 18 and 21). However, there are some particularly critical points that older people and their families and carers should bear in mind.

Eating and drinking

Eating and drinking properly are essential to an older person's recovery in hospital. They may not always receive the food and drink they need because of problems with sight, hearing or understanding – or simply because they have difficulty eating. If your loved one needs help to make menu choices, or assistance with eating and drinking, make sure staff are aware of this so that they can help. You should also let the staff know if the patient has preferences for particular types of food, or needs to eat at different times from the regular meals. If you want to bring in food for a relative or friend, this should be possible, but discuss this first with the nurse in charge in case the medical team or dieticians have advised a specific diet. Older patients should be weighed frequently when in hospital; if there are concerns about their weight or nutrition, a dietician will plan a special menu.

Make sure that staff are aware of any problems with chewing or swallowing (which are common as we get older). If these problems are severe, the staff will seek advice from expert therapists who will be able to make a full assessment and ensure the patient receives the most appropriate type and consistency of food. They will also be able to advise on the management of these problems once the person leaves hospital, and may refer them to similar therapists in the community.

Moving and walking

Keeping as active and independent as possible in hospital is very important for everyone, although this is obviously difficult when someone is very unwell. As soon as possible, though, older people will be encouraged – just as younger people are – to try to get out of bed. The nursing staff, physiotherapists and occupational therapists will work with them to help them regain their strength. It is important that they should remain as mobile as possible to maintain muscle strength, and to prevent pneumonia, pressure sores and blood clots in the veins. In hospital it can be all too easy to just stay in bed, but it is important to get up and move about as much as possible, for example by walking to the toilet rather than using a bed pan or commode. Patients often wonder why the doctors, nurses and physiotherapists keep 'nagging them' to get out of bed and walk; it is because staff are very aware that staying in bed is a threat to that person's long-term well-being and independence.

The physiotherapists and occupational therapists will assess the older person's needs as they recover, and work with them and the rest of the team to ensure that they have all the support they need on discharge from hospital.

Preventing falls

Older people are often admitted to hospital following a fall, but there is also a risk of falling while in hospital. There are many reasons why people fall, and older people who experience falls should be considered for referral to a falls prevention service. Most hospitals have specialist falls clinics, where the cause of falls or dizziness can be investigated. Keeping active in hospital is important, but preventing falls is even more important. Remembering to use glasses and walking aids, asking for help, and making sure the call bell is in reach can reduce the risk of falling.

Bladder and bowel care

Bladder and bowel function are often affected in older people during a hospital stay. Being unwell and being in hospital can lead to worsening of any existing problems with continence (whether affecting the bladder or bowel). Different medication (especially many painkillers), different routines and different food, and less mobility can often lead to constipation, which in turn can lead to pain, confusion, problems with bladder-emptying and a slower recovery. For these reasons, hospital staff will routinely ask about bowel habits. This can sometimes be embarrassing, but it is important that staff know if someone is experiencing problems so they can offer help. Laxatives, suppositories or even enemas can be prescribed if needed. Remember, though, that natural products in the diet can help too, such as dried fruit and certain drinks, including those with caffeine.

In certain scenarios, a catheter into the bladder may be required to drain urine. Catheters are avoided as much as possible as they increase the risk of urine infection, so the need for them should be reviewed on a daily basis. When a catheter is removed, it may take some time for bladder function to return to normal; do not be alarmed if this is the case.

Medication

Older people will often be taking several different kinds of medication. These drugs can sometimes interact with each other and produce side-effects. In addition to taking more medicines in general than most people, older people can also be more sensitive to any side-effects that do occur. The hospital team should therefore review all medication, making sure that they are all needed and that the patient understands what they are for and why they have been prescribed. It may be helpful to have a family member present during these discussions. Medication is often stopped or changed during a hospital stay once the staff have been able to make a full assessment of the patient's condition. The hospital doctors will write to the person's GP at the time of discharge from hospital so that any new medication can be continued, if necessary, when they return home. The patient should also be given a copy of this information, which they can share with their family, community pharmacist and other carers if they wish to do so.

If someone has trouble taking tablets – for instance, because of problems swallowing or remembering to take them – let the hospital staff know. A hospital pharmacist is likely to be the best person to help. The pharmacist may be able to change tablets to liquids, provide large-print labels, dispense tablets in an easy-to-open container, or provide a medicine reminder chart with details of the medication to be taken at each time of day clearly laid out. They may also assess the patient to see if some kind of medication box with compartments for different days and times would be helpful; however, these boxes are not the right solution for everyone as some medication cannot be put into the box and they can be fiddly to use.

Discharge planning, intermediate care and re-ablement services

The multidisciplinary team will regularly review each patient's progress and plan for discharge from hospital as soon as this is feasible. The team will, with permission, also communicate with the patient's relatives and carers. They will routinely ask about the older person's memory, walking ability, how they managed at home before their illness, and whether there were any problems with continence. The staff need to ensure that any problems that have not been identified up to that point are assessed, so that the necessary treatment can be given and the patient will receive the right kind of support after they leave hospital.

Sometimes a patient has recovered from their illness but needs more time and additional sessions with physiotherapists and occupational therapists to regain confidence in walking and being able to care for themselves. In these circumstances, the team may recommend that the older person spends some time in an 'intermediate care' or rehabilitation setting before returning home. At other times the team may consider that the rehabilitation therapy could better be provided at home; this is known as 're-ablement'.

If the older person is likely to need ongoing help with tasks such as washing, dressing or going to the toilet, the hospital team will arrange for this to be provided by social services on discharge. Sometimes a person may no longer be able to live independently and the team may recommend that they enter residential care or a nursing home.

Reassurance and support

Going into hospital is always a worrying experience, but knowing about how the hospital works and what to expect should make things a little easier. The key thing to remember is that there are people who can help if you are worried or uncertain about your relative's care. Visiting an older person in hospital is very helpful indeed; seeing a familiar and friendly face will be a great source of reassurance and support to your relative or friend.

CHAPTER TWENTY-FIVE

End of life care

The aim of healthcare is usually to restore or preserve health. However, when someone is near the end of their life, further treatment may not be beneficial and may even be burdensome. In these circumstances, doctors and patients together may choose not to give any further treatment. The focus of the clinical team then shifts from giving curative treatment to providing symptom relief and giving the person the best possible quality of life. Quality of life takes precedence over quantity. In this chapter we briefly consider some of the questions that may arise and decisions that may have to be made. Although these questions are potentially difficult and painful, reflecting on them and discussing them with family members should be helpful in creating a shared understanding of what may happen and making the best decisions for the person concerned.

Making decisions near the end of life

Any medical treatment can be declined by any adult patient as long as they are deemed to have the mental capacity to make that decision. Deciding whether or not to have treatment when the benefits are unclear is a very personal decision and dependent both on the person and their circumstances. An older person who feels that they have lived a good life and are ready to die may make a very different decision from a younger person who has a young family to support and wants to see them grow up. In all cases, the patient has a right to refuse treatment even if that refusal might hasten their death. The choices that doctors make near the end of their lives are very informative, because they understand the realities of treatment at that point in someone's life. Large studies have shown that doctors are far more likely to decline treatments towards the end of their lives than the rest of us, and are more likely to focus on receiving treatments which improve the quality of their lives than increase the duration.

Clinical teams have a responsibility to discuss the options fully and sensitively with the patient, but ultimately the decision rests with the patient. Some people decide that they do not want to discuss their illness in great detail; they prefer to leave decisions to others. In this case, clinical teams should only provide as much information as the patient would like. If someone does not have the mental capacity to make their own decisions, any decisions about their treatment will be first considered by the clinical team and then discussed with the patients' loved ones.

Some people make decisions in advance about their care around the end of their life. You may wish to consider doing this. This can help clinicians caring for you respect your wishes even if you are not conscious or able to discuss your wishes at the time. These advance decisions (sometimes known as a 'living will' or an 'advance directive') are decisions that you can make in advance to refuse a specific treatment at some point in the future. They set out what treatments you would be prepared to have and what treatment you would wish to refuse. Your family and clinical team can then be guided by this document if you are not able to make decisions yourself. An advance decision to refuse life-sustaining treatment in the future needs to be in writing, and signed by both the person concerned and an independent witness.

If the medical team feel that there is a possibility that a person may die within the next few days or hours, this should be communicated sensitively with the dying person and their family as soon as possible. According to current principles of palliative care, all decisions regarding treatment should be made with the involvement of the patient and those important to them. An individualised care plan including food and drink, symptom control, and psychological, social and spiritual support should be agreed, and then delivered with compassion.

Making advance decisions about resuscitation

A sudden cardiopulmonary arrest (see below) is extremely rare, either at home or in hospital. However, some people are at increased risk, including those with medical conditions such as terminal cancer or a life-threatening infection, and those who have recently had a heart attack or stroke. In such cases, the medical team looking after the patient may need to consider whether that person would want to be resuscitated if they have a cardiopulmonary arrest. Some people, particularly those who are already very ill or very elderly, may decide that they would rather not be resuscitated.

....

CPR is performed when someone has suffered a 'cardiopulmonary arrest', which means that their breathing or heart has stopped. The CPR process aims to restart the circulation and breathing with chest compressions. Electric shocks are sometimes also given to jolt the heart into a proper rhythm ('defibrillation') and sometimes injections of drugs. Although potentially life-saving, the process of CPR can itself cause injuries such as ribcage fractures or organ rupture. Even when CPR is successful, the patient may still require admission to an intensive care unit (ICU). Other types of treatment that may be needed after CPR include kidney dialysis, drugs to support the circulation, and other invasive procedures. A cardiopulmonary arrest requiring prolonged CPR can also mean that the brain becomes starved of oxygen, leading to permanent brain damage and potential long-term disability.

....

Any decision about resuscitation should be based on what is best for the individual concerned. The decision is sometimes straightforward, and sometimes more delicate and complex, for both patients and healthcare professionals. If someone is very clear that they would not wish to be resuscitated, or if the medical team consider that cardiopulmonary resuscitation (CPR) would be futile, then a 'do not attempt CPR' order, sometimes referred to as a 'do not attempt resuscitation order' or 'DNAR', will be documented at the front of their medical records. This must be signed and dated by the team member making the decision. The decision about resuscitation is the responsibility of the most senior healthcare professional (normally a consultant, GP, senior doctor in training or a senior nurse), but it can also be delegated to a more junior clinician if necessary. It is a legal requirement for the patient to be involved in the decision if at all possible.

The DNAR decision only applies to the particular circumstance of a sudden cardiopulmonary arrest. The patient and their family should not worry that any other aspect of their treatment will be affected by this decision. A person who has requested DNAR status will continue to be cared for to the same high standard as before the decision.

If a patient insists that resuscitation should be attempted if needed, despite it being unlikely to succeed, the clinician will ensure that they have provided information about the nature of resuscitation and the possible adverse outcomes. If a patient is still clear that they wish to be resuscitated, even after being informed of the risks, then these wishes will be respected and they will be resuscitated if they have an arrest. If someone states that they do not want CPR despite the clinicians' belief that it would have a high chance of being successful, the healthcare professionals will again discuss this with the patient. If the patient still refuses CPR, their wish will also be respected.

Options for care at the end of life

Palliative care aims to maintain or improve a person's quality of life in the last days of their life. Palliative care includes support for the patient's loved ones, who are recognised as needing help in their own right and being part of the team who are caring for the patient.

When someone is nearing the end of their life, there are several options for how and where their care takes place:

Hospice care

The modern hospice movement can be attributed to a remarkable British nurse turned doctor, Dame Cicely Saunders. She spent many years tirelessly fundraising, training and establishing the hospice movement. In 1967 she founded the world's first hospice, St Christopher's Hospice in south-west London. She revolutionised the concept and culture of the specialty dedicated to caring for terminally ill people: palliative care.

Every year hospices care for over 250,000 people in Britain, both in the hospice setting itself and by providing support in people's homes. Hospice care is for people with terminal illnesses; this includes cancer, but also other conditions such as dementia or organ failure. The care provided in hospices is not simply focused on the medical management of these diseases. There is a strong focus on holistic care, which means supporting people's social, emotional, spiritual and financial needs, as well as the needs of their loved ones.

A common misconception is that a hospice admission means that a person will die there. For two thirds of people, this is not the case. Only one third of admissions to hospices are for the patient to receive terminal care. Some people are even discharged from the service if their needs have been met, although they can always return if necessary.

Care in a person's own home

Palliative care does not have to take place in a hospice. There are also community-based teams to support people who wish to remain at home. These teams offer help with symptom control, and can give emotional and practical support as well as helping carers and families. The community palliative care team work alongside GPs and community nurses. Hospices may also offer day care, which provides people with the benefits of hospice care without the need to stay overnight. Day care support means that people can continue living at home, while having access to medical care and complementary therapies and opportunities to meet other people.

The amount of support that people can receive at home varies across the country and according to the illness a person has. There are a number of very valuable organisations which provide care at home, the best-known being the Macmillan and Marie Curie nurses (see Appendix). Macmillan nurses provide specialist advice regarding symptom control (such as pain and nausea) for patients with cancer and other conditions, as well as emotional support to patients and their families throughout the illness. Marie Curie nurses provide support towards the end of someone's life, in the last few weeks or months. They offer nursing care, and can provide care overnight. Any organisation providing care at home should communicate regularly with patients and their family, the patient's GP and the hospital to coordinate and optimise care.

Coming to terms with the death of a loved one

For many of us, bereavement is the most psychologically distressing experience that we will face. When someone close to us dies, we have to adjust to a world that seems to have changed completely. In the immediate aftermath people often describe feeling numbness, disbelief or disorientation. In addition to the pain of the loss, the bereaved may feel very angry at times, due to a sense of unfairness or cruelty, for example. There may be feelings of guilt about what was said or not said to the person who has died, and periods of depression and hopelessness. Everyone experiences grief differently and there is no right way to grieve. How individuals react will be influenced by many things, including their age, personality, cultural background and religious beliefs, previous experiences of bereavement and personal circumstances. The nature of the death in question can also play a part, particularly if the death was sudden or unexpected.

The distress of the first weeks of bereavement can be made worse by having to deal with the many practical issues surrounding death, which can at times feel bewildering and overwhelming. Most of us are completely unaware of the formalities and processes involved until we experience the death of someone close to us. The UK government has some helpful guidance which is available online (see Appendix).

The support of family and friends during bereavement makes a huge difference to most of us, and most people gradually emerge from the bereavement process. However, when a bereavement seems particularly difficult and the bereaved person seems unable to recover from the loss, it is important to consider professional help. There are a number of support facilities to help the bereaved through their grief, including Cruse Bereavement Care, Hope Again (for young people) and the Bereavement Services Association. Cruse is committed to ensuring that everyone, no matter how old or young, can access the highest quality support following a bereavement. Cruse offers telephone and on-line support. Trained volunteers in its branches across the UK provide face-to-face practical advice and support. Hope Again is a website developed by Cruse to support young people after the death of someone close to them.

Leaving
hospital

CHAPTER TWENTY-SIX

Leaving hospital

We wanted the book to finish on a positive note and this is why the last chapter is all about leaving hospital, or 'being discharged'. Being discharged from hospital may sound rather alarming, but it simply means that arrangements are being made for you to leave. The professionals looking after you believe that you no longer need the expertise and levels of care provided in hospital. Put simply, you are getting better.

Leaving hospital after a brief stay is normally quite straight-forward. It can, however, be more complicated and sometimes more worrying for patients who have been seriously ill or who have been in hospital for some weeks. The hospital has become a familiar place of safety and the reassuring presence of clinical staff gives both patients and family a sense of security.

Many factors are taken into account when planning your dis-charge from hospital. These include the reason you were admit-ted, how much your overall condition has changed during your time in hospital, and your living arrangements and the support available to you at home. In all cases, the staff looking after you should discuss the discharge process with you, and where appro-priate with your family as well. The aim is to make leaving a safe, secure process and to avoid, wherever possible, you having to return to hospital for 're-admission'.

Preparing to leave hospital

Planning discharge at the very start of an admission can seem strange to people who are unfamiliar with hospitals. However, doing so focuses both the clinical team and the patient on the key goal of leaving hospital. It also helps to minimise any delays once you are ready to go home.

Estimated discharge date

Discharge planning has improved significantly in recent times and clinical staff will often give you an estimated discharge date as soon as you arrive in hospital. For instance, if you are having a routine operation, they will know how long you are likely to need to stay. Thinking ahead in this way helps the staff plan your stay in hospital, and helps you and your family plan your return home. The estimated discharge date can of course be adjusted; you can leave earlier if you recover quickly, or stay longer if you need to.

When will I be ready to go home?

You are ready for discharge when you no longer need care, treatment or tests that only a hospital can provide. If your hospital treatment has finished, you are able to walk without assistance, and you can wash, prepare meals and go to the toilet unaided, you are probably ready to go home. If you still need help with these things, or require some other care (wound management, for example), the clinical team may discuss other options with you and your family. These are set out later in the chapter.

Who might be involved in my discharge planning?

If you have been admitted to hospital for a routine planned operation, such as a small hernia repair, a doctor will decide when you can go home and a nurse or discharge coordinator will make the necessary arrangements. However if, at the other extreme, you have spent two months in hospital with a very serious condition, much more planning is needed and many people may be involved (see Table 6).

Table 6 Staff involved in the discharge process

Staff member	Roles in discharge planning
Discharge coordinator	Coordinates the process of assessment and discharge; helps complete relevant paperwork
Doctor	Makes the decision about whether a patient is ready to be discharged; arranges any necessary medical follow-up or transition to the care of doctors elsewhere
Ward nursing staff	Usually in overall charge of the discharge process, assessing future nursing needs, communicating actively with patients and their carers
Physiotherapist	Assesses physical abilities such as transferring from bed to chair and managing stairs; arranges physiotherapy in a community setting if necessary
Occupational therapist	Assesses functional capabilities such as washing and dressing, making meals; provides specialist equipment to assist people at home
Pharmacist	Checks that the discharge prescription is appropriate; prepares medication ready for discharge; explains medication to patients and carers; helps communicate details of medication changes to patients and their GPs
Social worker	Provides support with financial matters and living arrangements; suggests how these needs can be met and funded; coordinates carers
District nurse	Arranges nursing in a person's own home or in a residential home, perhaps including assistance with catheter care, pressure sores, leg ulcers and wound dressings

At the end of your hospital stay

Final discharge decisions are often made first thing in the morning, when your doctor reviews your progress during the morning ward round. Once you know you are going home, there may be a delay while discharge summaries are completed, a supply of medication is organised and transport is arranged. During this period you may be asked to wait in another area of the hospital (the discharge lounge) rather than staying on the ward. This allows your bed space to be prepared for the next patient and improves the flow of patients through the hospital.

What if I disagree with the discharge plan?

Discharge plans are always made in consultation with patients and their family or carers, so it is only rarely that there are disagreements between the patient and their hospital team. However, if you disagree strongly with what is being proposed, you must discuss this with the hospital team. If there is a misunderstanding, plans can be changed.

What do I do if I feel that I need to stay longer in hospital?

A doctor may decide that someone is ready to go home even though the person concerned feels that they need to stay in hospital for longer. Generally this is because the staff know that being as active and independent as possible is the best route to recovery; staying in hospital too long can make you weaker and prolong your recovery. However, doctors can also underestimate how much support someone needs to continue getting better. If you really feel that you are not ready to go home, you and your family must make this clear. The best person to speak to initially is usually the senior nurse on your ward.

What do I do if I want to leave early or discharge myself from hospital?

An alternative problem is that you decide that you want to leave hospital but the staff advise you to remain. Once again, the most important thing is to discuss this carefully and fully with the hospital staff. Sometimes patients wish to discharge themselves from hospital because they have not fully understood the seriousness of their condition, or have misunderstood the treatment that is planned. In these situations, the doctors and nurses need to explain clearly why it is in your best interests to stay.

Patients are in fact free to leave hospital at any point. Only in exceptional circumstances, such as when people are a risk to themselves or others, can a person be held against their will. In general, you are free to leave even if your doctors advise against it. This is called 'discharge against medical advice'. It is very rare that patients discharge themselves against medical advice, but it is nevertheless important to know that this is your right.

If you do decide to leave against medical advice, you have to go through a formal process. The doctor has a legal duty to check that you have the capacity to understand the potential consequences of your decision. This is to protect people who may be temporarily disturbed from taking decisions that they may regret later. For instance, someone might be delirious but also have a physical problem. They would not be permitted to leave if their doctors considered that they were incapable of making a rational decision.

If you decide to discharge yourself and your doctor agrees that you understand what you are doing, then you can leave. You will be asked to sign a form confirming your decision to act against medical advice. The process will be made as safe as possible, and your GP will receive a letter explaining the tests and treatment you have had and describing the circumstances in which you left hospital.

Returning home after being in hospital

You will be eager to get home after your hospital stay, but before you leave it is important to make sure you have enough support on the journey, and that you understand how your treatment will continue at home.

How will I get home?

You may feel well enough to travel home independently after a short stay in hospital. However, it is almost always best that someone accompanies you. If you have undergone sedation (for a procedure such as an endoscopy or a biopsy) or have had a general anaesthetic, you should not drive. In these circumstances, you should also ask someone to be with you for 24 hours after you return home. This is partly so that they can look after you, but also so that they can contact your doctor if you do not recover as quickly as expected. Occasionally patients require more specialised transport or do not have anyone available to help them get home. Hospital transport or an ambulance can be arranged to take you home if it is difficult for you to make other arrangements.

What about my medicines? Will my GP know about any changes?

Your GP will be sent a letter summarising the reasons for your admission to hospital and the tests and treatments you received. This important letter is called a 'discharge summary' and is the main way the hospital staff communicate with your GP at the end of your stay. You should also receive a copy of this letter for your own records, either given to you or posted to your home address.

Your doctors will prescribe any medicines you need to continue taking when you get home. These medicines will be dispensed together with instructions from the hospital pharmacy, and given to you before you leave. The discharge summary will include a list of the medicines that you have been given and will inform your GP about any medicines they need to prescribe for you in the future. Before you leave, you should make sure that you are clear about any new medicines that have been prescribed and how long you will need to take them for, and about any that have been stopped (and why).

Continuing your recovery at home

Patients sometimes believe that they will only be discharged when they are feeling fully well. This is not necessarily the case and it is not in your best interests to stay in hospital any longer than necessary. You will be discharged when you no longer need all the support and treatments that a hospital provides. Once you get to that point, you will recover much more quickly at home; there you can be active, be among family and friends, and return to your ordinary life.

After a serious illness or major operation you may well continue to have some symptoms, such as mild pain, tiredness, loss of appetite, altered bowel habits or altered sleep. You may need to adapt to changes to your everyday life, such as home oxygen, catheters, walking aids, stomas or new diets. If you have had surgery, your wounds may require dressing. All this requires adjustment and can be stressful until you become accustomed to the changes. Both going into hospital and returning home can be major events in some people's lives.

Your rehabilitation will therefore continue long after you leave hospital. You need to be kind to yourself and realise that you may need to take things slowly for a few weeks. Additional services may be organised to provide essential care and to speed your recovery (see Table 7).

If you are not recovering as expected or you are concerned about what is happening, you must seek advice. Patients are frequently discharged with the telephone number of a nurse

Table 7 Additional support at home

Destination on leaving hospital	Who is the support for?	Who will provide extra support?
Home with extra social support	People who need practical help with shopping, meals brought to them, or daily assistance with washing and dressing	Family members or friends Private carers Carers funded by social services
Home with specialised therapists, nurses or carers	People who are able to manage safely at home but need additional clinical support (such as wound dressing or help to improve mobility) during their recovery	This depends on locally-provided services, but may include: – hospital therapists who visit people in their own homes after discharge; – community-based physiotherapists who visit people to improve their physical ability or help with day-to-day tasks such as using the toilet unaided; – district nurses to supervise medication or care of wounds; – social services carers to help with daily living.

specialist from the team that was looking after them. Your GP is another good source of expertise and support. Advice is often available on the internet too, although you should be careful only to use trustworthy sources of advice. There is a list of useful and reliable websites in the Appendix at the back of this book.

Moving to another type of hospital or a nursing home

There are times when a person's illness or condition means they will not be able to return to living independently. This can obviously be upsetting for both the patient and their family, but is sometimes necessary if the patient is to receive the continuing care they require. These new arrangements may be temporary or permanent. There are increasing efforts to support patients in their homes, but sheltered accommodation, community hospitals and care homes will be needed for some people (see Table 8).

Table 8 Rehabilitation, nursing and care homes

Destination on leaving hospital	Who is the service for?	Who will provide it?
Community hospitals and dedicated rehabilitation units	People who are well enough to leave hospital but who need a period of rehabilitation that cannot be provided at home. Some may need care overnight because they would not be safe in their home environment	Professional carers and nurses provide care. GPs or hospital doctors may visit regularly. Therapists provide rehabilitation. Staff are on site 24 hours a day.
Residential care homes	People who are unable to manage at home any longer, but can walk and look after themselves	Carers are available 24 hours a day. GPs or hospital doctors visit regularly.
Nursing care homes	People who are unable to manage at home any longer and who also need nursing care	Nurses are available 24 hours a day. GPs or hospital doctors visit regularly.

Discharge to a care home

If a person is no longer able to care for themselves, and needs relatively high levels of support, they may need to be looked after in a care home. Most people choose to move to a care home (either 'residential' or 'nursing') near where they were living before, although it is also possible to move to a different area so that you can be near your family. A social worker can help by providing you with a list of appropriate homes that you, your family or friends can visit and assess. If you are not able to visit any, the social worker will help you choose a care home.

Funding additional care

If you require extra care when you are discharged, whether it is increased personal care at home or a move to a care home, there will probably be financial implications. Your social worker and the discharge coordinator will explain what support is available to help fund your care. The extent of the support available will depend on your assets and what care you need, for what duration and in what setting. Your social worker will guide you through the completion of relevant forms, which may well involve your partner, family members and your next of kin. Further information is available from Age UK and other organisations listed in the Appendix at the back of this book.

A final word

At the beginning of this book we compared the hospital to a foreign land as a way of conveying the sense of bewilderment and confusion that many people feel when they go into hospital. We explained that we saw this book as being like a travel guide in explaining the activities, customs, organisation and language of a hospital as well as describing the main types of investigations and treatment. We hope the book helps you make the best decisions for you and your family, makes the overall experience more comprehensible, and helps you look after yourself and others during the hospital journey.

Appendix

Useful sources of information

There are many organisations who dedicate themselves to the support of patients, families and carers with particular illnesses, or who provide more general information about healthcare. Below we highlight some organisations that we particularly recommend, and their websites.

General sources of advice

NHS Choices
www.nhs.uk
Provides information from the UK National Health Service on conditions, treatments, local services and healthy living

Healthwatch England
www.healthwatch.co.uk
The independent consumer champion for health and social care in England, which aims to develop new ways of engaging and informing people, especially those who sometimes struggle to be heard

Patient.co.uk
www.patient.co.uk
An online medical resource, supplying patients with evidence-based information on a wide range of medical and health topics

The Patients Association
www.patients-association.org.uk
A charity advocating better information for patients and the public, equal access to high-quality healthcare for patients,

and the right for patients to be involved in all aspects of decision-making

Scotland Patients' Association
www.scotlandpatients.com
Provides support and information for all those using services delivered by hospitals or in the community in Scotland

Patient Advice and Support Service Scotland (PASS)
www.patientadvicescotland.org.uk
An independent service providing free, accessible and confidential information, advice and support to patients, their carers and families in relation to NHS healthcare in Scotland

Patient and Client Council (Northern Ireland)
www.patientclientcouncil.hscni.net
Promotes a health and social care service in Northern Ireland that is shaped by patients, clients, carers and communities

Community Health Councils in Wales
www.patienthelp.wales.nhs.uk
Provides help and advice if you have problems with NHS services in Wales, or wish to complain; ensures that patients' views and needs influence healthcare policy

Specific illnesses and treatments

Diabetes UK
www.diabetes.org.uk
The leading diabetes charity in the UK; cares for, connects with and campaigns on behalf of all people affected by and at risk of diabetes

British Heart Foundation
www.bhf.org.uk
The major heart charity in the UK and the largest independent funder of cardiovascular research, providing extensive patient information

Mencap
www.mencap.org.uk
The leading voice of learning disability, supporting people with a learning disability and their families and carers

Stroke Association
www.stroke.org.uk
Provides support for stroke survivors, campaigns for better stroke prevention and care, and funds research into stroke

Alzheimer's Society
www.alzheimers.org.uk
A membership organisation working to improve the quality of life of people affected by dementia across the UK

UK Sepsis Trust
http://sepsistrust.org
Provides support for those affected by the scale and significance of the impact of severe sepsis on sufferers and their families

ICUsteps
www.icusteps.org
Provides support for patients, families and relatives affected by critical illness

NHS Blood and Transplant
www.blood.co.uk
Scottish National Blood Transfusion Service
www.scotblood.co.uk
Welsh Blood Service
www.welsh-blood.org.uk
Northern Ireland Blood Transfusion Service
www.nibts.org
The collection of blood and subsequent dissemination to hospitals and clinics is delivered by four different organisations in the UK, dependent on location. Each organisation, on its website, gives important information about donating and receiving blood.

Anthony Nolan Trust
www.anthonynolan.org
Provides support for patients with blood cancer

Cancer Research UK
www.cancerresearchuk.org
A major funder of research into cancer in the UK; provides extensive information about cancer

Macmillan Cancer Support
www.macmillan.org.uk
Provides information and support for people with cancer

Breast Cancer Now
www.breastcancernow.org
The UK's leading breast cancer charity

Roy Castle Lung Cancer Foundation
www.roycastle.org
The UK's only lung cancer charity, committed to medical research, reducing smoking and patient support

Bowel Cancer UK
www.bowelcanceruk.org.uk
Works to save lives and improve the quality of life for all those affected by bowel cancer

Intensive Care Society (ICS)
www.ics.ac.uk
Represents intensive care professionals and patients in the UK; provides information for patients and families, and accounts of the experience of intensive care

Staying well in hospital

Infection Prevention Society
www.ips.uk.net
Seeks to protect patients from preventable infections by working with patients and staff in all healthcare settings

Thrombosis UK
www.thrombosis-charity.org.uk
Promotes awareness of thrombosis, as well as research and care

Support for older people

Age UK
www.ageuk.org.uk
The UK's largest charity working with and for older people

Royal Voluntary Service
www.royalvoluntaryservice.org.uk
A volunteer organisation that supports and enriches the lives of older people and their families across the UK

End of life care and bereavement

Marie Curie
www.mariecurie.org.uk
Cares for people with any terminal illness and their families, offering expert care, guidance and support to help people make the most of the time that remains to them

Together for Short Lives
www.togetherforshortlives.org.uk
The leading UK charity for children with life-threatening and life-limiting conditions, and all those who support, love and care for them

Cruse Bereavement Care
www.cruse.org.uk
An organisation that people can turn to for help, support and guidance when someone important to them dies

Hope Again
www.hopeagain.org.uk
The youth website of Cruse Bereavement Care, a safe place for young people facing grief to share their stories and gain support from others

Government Bereavement Advice
www.gov.uk/after-a-death/overview
Provides practical information and support after someone dies

Bereavement Services Association
www.bsauk.org
An association that works across all types of organisations to promote excellence in the care of dying people

Lightning Source UK Ltd.
Milton Keynes UK
UKOW06f1244140817
307195UK00008B/159/P